Cambridge Latin Course
SECOND EDITION

Unit IVA

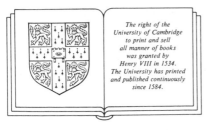

The right of the
University of Cambridge
to print and sell
all manner of books
was granted by
Henry VIII in 1534.
The University has printed
and published continuously
since 1584.

CAMBRIDGE UNIVERSITY PRESS

Cambridge

New York   Port Chester

Melbourne   Sydney

Published by the Press Syndicate of the University of Cambridge
The Pitt Building, Trumpington Street, Cambridge CB2 1RP
40 West 20th Street, New York, NY 10011, USA
10 Stamford Road, Oakleigh, Melbourne 3166, Australia

This book, an outcome of work jointly commissioned by the Schools
Council before its closure and the Cambridge School Classics Project, is
published under the aegis of the School Curriculum Development
Committee, Newcombe House, 45 Notting Hill Gate, London W11 3JB.

First published 1971
Seventh printing 1982
Second edition 1986
Reprinted 1990

Printed in the United States of America

ISBN 0 521 27438 9
ISBN 0 521 31278 7 North American edition

Thanks are due to the following for permission to reproduce photographs:
p15 Ashmolean Museum, Oxford; p22 Fototeca Unione, at the American
Academy in Rome; p33 Colchester and Essex Museum; pp 34, 52, 75, 97, 119
The Mansell Collection; p45 Instituto Centrale per il Catalogo e la
Documentazione (ICCD); p63 Roger Dalladay; p73 The Trustees of the
British Museum; p99 from C. Brower and J. Masen, *Antiquitatum Treuerensium
libri xxv* (1670); p121 phot. Bibliothèque Nationale, Paris

Drawings by Peter Kesteven, Joy Mellor and Leslie Jones
Plan by Reg Piggott

Contents

rūs

When you have read this, answer the questions at the end.

ex urbe

Mānius Acīlius Glabriō salūtem dīcit Lupō amīcō.
quid agis, mī Lupe, in vīllā tuā rūsticā? iamne ex istō morbō
convaluistī? quid agit Helvidius, fīlius tuus?

    quotiēns dē tē tuāque vīllā cōgitō, tibi valdē invideō; nam in urbe
nūllum est ōtium, nūlla quiēs. ego quidem multīs negōtiīs cotīdiē 5
occupātus sum. prīmā hōrā ā clientibus meīs salūtor; inde ad
basilicam vel cūriam contendō; aliquandō amīcōs vīsitō, vel ab eīs
vīsitor; per tōtum diem officia prīvāta vel pūblica agō. at tū intereā
in rīpā flūminis vel in umbrā arboris ōtiōsus fortasse iacēs, et dum
ego strepitū urbis vexor, tū carmine avium dēlectāris. sed satis 10
querēlārum!

quid agis? *how are you? how are you getting on?*
invideō: invidēre *envy*
ōtium *leisure*
prīvāta: prīvātus *private*
arboris: arbor *tree*
querēlārum: querēla *complaint*

'**dum ego strepitū urbis vexor, tū carmine avium dēlectāris.**' (lines 9–10)

Imperātor Domitiānus triumphum heri dē Germānīs ēgit. pompa, per tōtam urbem prōgressa, ā multīs laudābātur, ā nōnnūllīs dērīdēbātur. aliī 'spectāculum splendidissimum!'
15 clāmābant. 'Imperātor noster, pater vērus patriae, gentēs barbarās iam superāvit; Germānī per viās urbis iam in triumphō dūcuntur!' aliī tamen 'spectāculum rīdiculum!' susurrābant. 'illī quī per viās dūcuntur haudquāquam Germānī sunt, sed servī, ex prōvinciā Hispāniā arcessītī et veste Germānā indūtī! ēn splendidus
20 Imperātor quī, paucīs homunculīs victīs, sē dignum triumphō putat!'

litterae cotīdiē ā Britanniā exspectantur, ubi Agricola bellum contrā Calēdoniōs gerit. Calēdoniī crēduntur ferōcissimī omnium Britannōrum esse. dē Calēdoniā ipsā omnīnō incertus sum, mī
25 Lupe. utrum pars est Britanniae an īnsula sēiūncta?

ad cōnsilium Imperātōris adesse saepe iubeor. invītus pāreō; quotiēns enim sententiam meam ā Domitiānō rogor, difficile est mihi respondēre; turpe vidētur mentīrī, perīculōsum vēra loquī. nūper ego et aliī senātōrēs ab Imperātōre cōnsultī sumus dē poenā
30 illārum Virginum Vestālium quae incestī damnātae erant. supplicium ultimum eīs dēcrēvimus; magnum erat eārum scelus, et merita poena. at cōgitā impudentiam Domitiānī! Virginēs enim ob incestum sevērē pūnit, ipse vītam impūrissimam vīvit.

audīvistīne umquam poētam Valerium Mārtiālem recitantem?
35 ego quidem recitātiōnibus eius saepe adsum; tū sī eum audīveris, certē dēlectāberis. versūs eius semper ēlegantēs, nōnnumquam scurrīlēs sunt. eum tamen ideō reprehendō, quod Imperātōrem nimium adulātur.

quandō rūre discēdēs, mī Lupe? quandō iterum tē in urbe
40 vidēbimus? cum prīmum ad urbem redierīs, mē vīsitā, quaesō; sī tē mox vīderō, valdē dēlectābor. valē.

triumphum . . . ēgit: triumphum agere *celebrate a triumph*
dē Germānīs *over the Germans*
patriae: patria *country, homeland*
veste: vestis *clothing*
indūtī: indūtus *dressed*
litterae *letters, correspondence*
Calēdoniōs: Calēdoniī *Scots*
utrum . . . est . . . an? *is it . . . or?*
sēiūncta: sēiūnctus *separate*
cōnsilium *council*
turpe: turpis *shameful*
mentīrī *lie, tell a lie*
incestī: incestum *immorality, unchastity*
supplicium ultimum *death penalty*
dēcrēvimus: dēcernere *vote, decree*
impudentiam: impudentia *shamelessness*
ob *on account of, because of*
impūrissimam: impūrus *immoral*
recitātiōnibus: recitātiō *recital, public reading*
nōnnumquam *sometimes*
ideo . . . quod *for the reason that, because*
reprehendō: reprehendere *blame, criticise*
adulātur: adulārī *flatter*
cum prīmum *as soon as*
quaesō *I beg, i.e. please*

1 Who is the writer of this letter? To whom is it written? Where are they both?
2 Why does Glabrio envy Lupus? What does he imagine Lupus is doing while Glabrio is working?
3 What public event has just taken place in Rome? Why have some Romans regarded it as ridiculous?
4 From where, and from whom, is news expected? What has Glabrio heard about the Scots?
5 What request does Glabrio often receive from the Emperor? Why does he dislike obeying this request? Whose punishment has recently been discussed by the Emperor's advisers? Does Glabrio feel that the punishment was justified? Why does he feel indignant about it?
6 Whose public readings has Glabrio been attending? What criticism does he make of him?
7 What does Glabrio finally ask Lupus, and what request does he make?

Language note

1 Study the following examples:

māne ā clientibus meīs **salūtor**.
In the morning, I am greeted by my clients.

amīcum prōdidistī; rēctē nunc **pūnīris**.
You betrayed your friend; now you are rightly punished.

The words in heavy print are *passive* forms of the 1st and 2nd persons singular.

2 Compare the active and passive forms of the 1st person singular in the following three tenses:

	active	*passive*
present	portō	portor
	I carry	I am carried
future	portābō	portābor
	I shall carry	I shall be carried
imperfect	portābam	portābar
	I was carrying	I was being carried

Further examples:

1 laudor, laudābor, laudābar; doceor, docēbor, docēbar.
2 mittor, impedior, appellor; superābor, terrēbor, invītābor; prohibēbar, incitābar, trahēbar.

3 Compare the active and passive forms of the 2nd person singular:

	active	*passive*
present	portās	portāris
	you carry	you are carried
future	portābis	portāberis
	you will carry	you will be carried
imperfect	portābās	portābāris
	you were carrying	you were being carried

Further examples:

1 culpāris, culpāberis; culpābāris; iubēris, iubēberis, iubēbāris.
2 spectāris, audīris, monēris; rogāberis, docēberis; neglegēbāris, salūtābāris.

4 Further examples of 1st and 2nd person forms:

1 nōlī dēspērāre! mox līberāberis.
2 nunc ab omnibus laudor; anteā ab omnibus culpābar.
3 herī in carcere retinēbāris; hodiē ab Imperātōre honōrāris.
4 vexor, vexāris; audiēbar, audiēbāris; dērīdēbor, dērīdēberis.

5 Compare the passive forms in paragraphs 2 and 3 with the forms of the deponent verb 'cōnor':

present	cōnor	I try	cōnāris	you try
future	cōnābor	I shall try	cōnāberis	you will try
imperfect	cōnābar	I was trying	cōnābāris	you were trying

Further examples of 1st and 2nd person forms of deponent verbs:

1 cūr domum meam ingrediēbāris?
2 crās deam precābor.
3 polliceor, pollicēris; cōnspicābor, cōnspicāberis; sequēbar, sequēbāris.

vīta rūstica

C. Helvidius Lupus salūtem dīcit Acīliō Glabriōnī amīcō.
cum epistulam tuam legerem, mī Glabriō, gaudium et dolōrem
simul sēnsī. gaudiō enim afficiēbar, quod tam diū epistulam ā tē
exspectābam; dolēbam autem, quod tū tot labōribus opprimēbāris.
5   in epistulā tuā dīcis tē valdē occupātum esse. ego quoque, cum
Rōmae essem, saepe negōtiīs vexābar; nunc tamen vītā rūsticā
fruor, aliquandō per agrōs meōs equitō; aliquandō fundum īnspiciō.
crās in silvīs proximīs vēnābor; vīcīnī enim crēdunt aprum
ingentem ibi latēre. nōn tamen omnīnō ōtiōsus sum; nam sīcut tū ā
10 clientibus tuīs salūtāris atque vexāris, ita ego ā colōnīs meīs assiduē
vexor.
    simulatque ad hanc vīllam advēnī, medicum quendam, quī prope
habitābat, arcessīvī; morbō enim valdē afflīgēbar. medicus mē iussit
vīnō abstinēre, medicīnamque sūmere. septem continuōs diēs ā
15 medicō vīsitābar; morbus intereā ingravēscēbat. octāvō diē
medicum dīmīsī, vīnum bibere coepī, medicīnam in cloācam effūdī.
statim convaluī.
    rēctē dīcis Calēdoniōs omnium Britannōrum ferōcissimōs esse.
amīcus meus Silānus, quī cum Agricolā in Britanniā nūper
20 mīlitābat, dīcit Calēdoniōs in ultimīs partibus Britanniae habitāre,
inter saxa et undās. quamquam Calēdoniī ferōcissimē pugnāre
solent, Silānus cōnfīdit exercitum nostrum eōs vincere posse. crēdit
enim Rōmānōs nōn modo fortiōrēs esse quam Calēdoniōs, sed etiam
ducem meliōrem habēre.
25   dē poētā Mārtiāle tēcum cōnsentiō: inest in eō multum ingenium,
multa ars. ego vērō ōlim versibus Ovidiī poētae maximē dēlectābar;
nunc tamen mihi epigrammata Mārtiālis magis placent.
    in epistulā tuā Helvidium, fīlium meum, commemorās. quem
tamen rārissimē videō! nam in hāc vīllā trēs diēs mēcum morātus,
30 ad urbem rediit; suspicor eum puellam aliquam in urbe vīsitāre.
quīndecim iam annōs nātus est; nihil cūrat nisi puellās et quadrīgās.
difficile autem est mihi eum castīgāre; nam ego quoque, cum iuvenis
essem – sed satis dē hīs nūgīs.

8

'**sīcut tū ā clientibus tuīs salūtāris atque vexāris, ita ego ā colōnīs meīs assiduē vexor.'** (lines 9–11)

nunc tū mihi graviter admonendus es, mī Glabriō. in epistulā tuā identidem dē quōdam virō potentī male scrībis, quem nōmināre 35 nōlō. tibi cavendum est, mī amīce! perīculōsum est dē potentibus male scrībere. virī potentēs celeriter īrāscuntur, lentē molliuntur. haec tibi ideō dīcō, quod patris meī cārissimī memor sum; quī cum Vespasiānum Imperātōrem offendisset, prīmum relēgātus, deinde occīsus est. nisi cāverīs, mī Glabriō, tū quoque, sicut pater meus, 40 damnāberis atque occīderis. sollicitus haec scrībō; salūs enim tua mihi magnae cūrae est. valē.

dolēbam: dolēre *grieve, be sad*
fruor: fruī *enjoy*
vēnābor: vēnārī *hunt*
vīcīnī: vīcīnus *neighbour*
sīcut . . . ita *just as . . . so*
colōnīs: colōnus *tenant-farmer*
abstinēre *abstain*
sūmere *take*
cloācam: cloāca *drain*
cōnfīdit: cōnfīdere *be sure, be confident*

vērō *indeed*
epigrammata: epigramma *epigram*
aliquam: aliquī *some*
quadrīgās: quadrīga *chariot*
nūgīs: nūgae *nonsense, foolish talk*
admonendus es: admonēre *warn, advise*
male *badly, unfavourably*
nōmināre *name, mention by name*
īrāscuntur: īrāscī *become angry*

Exercises

1 Match each adjective in the left-hand column with an adjective of the opposite meaning, taken from the right-hand column, and translate both words.

For example: absēns absent   praesēns present

absēns	parvus
dīves	multī
laetus	vīvus
longus	bonus
magnus	praesēns
malus	trīstis
mortuus	antīquus
novus	vacuus
paucī	brevis
plēnus	pauper

2 Complete each sentence with the most suitable verb from the list below, using the correct form, and then translate. Do not use any verb more than once.

terrēbit	reficiet	dabit	certābit	dūcet
terrēbunt	reficient	dabunt	certābunt	dūcent

1 hī fabrī sunt perītissimī; nāvem tuam celeriter . . . .
2 crās dominus lībertātem duōbus servīs . . . .
3 leōnēs, quī ferōciōrēs sunt quam cēterae bēstiae, spectātōrēs fortasse . . . .
4 sī templum vīsitāre vīs, hic servus tē illūc . . . .
5 frāter meus, aurīga nōtissimus, crās in Circō Maximō . . . .

3 With the help of paragraph 8 on page 134 of the Language Information section, turn each of the following pairs into one sentence by replacing the word in heavy print with the correct form of the relative pronoun 'quī', and then translate.

For example: prō templō erant duo tribūnī. **tribūnōs** statim agnōvī.

This becomes: prō templō erant duo tribūnī, quōs statim agnōvī.

In front of the temple were two tribunes, whom I recognised at once.

1 in fundō nostrō sunt vīgintī servī. **servī** in agrīs cotīdiē labōrant.
2 prope iānuam stābat nūntius. **nūntiō** epistulam trādidī.
3 in hāc vīllā habitat lībertus. **lībertum** vīsitāre volō.
4 audī illam puellam! **puella** suāviter cantat.
5 in viā erant multī puerī. **puerōrum** clāmōrēs senem vexābant.

Language note

1 In Unit I, you met sentences like these:

'mercātor multam pecūniam habet.'
'The merchant has a lot of money.'

'servī fraudem parant.'
'The slaves are preparing a trick.'

In each example, a statement is being *made*. These examples are known as *direct* statements. Notice the nouns 'mercātor' and 'servī' and the verbs 'habet' and 'parant'.

2 In Stage 35, you have met sentences like these:

scīmus **mercātōrem** multam pecūniam **habēre**.
We know the merchant to have a lot of money.
    or, in more natural English:
We know that the merchant has a lot of money.

crēdō **servōs** fraudem **parāre**.
I believe the slaves to be preparing a trick.
    or, in more natural English:
I believe that the slaves are preparing a trick.

In each of these examples, the statement is not being made, but is being *reported* or *mentioned*. These examples are known as *indirect* statements. Notice that the nouns 'mercātōrem' and 'servōs' are now in the *accusative* case, and the verbs 'habēre' and 'parāre' are now in the *infinitive* form.

3 Compare the following examples:

direct statements	*indirect statements*
'captīvī dormiunt.'	centuriō dīcit **captīvōs dormīre**.
'The prisoners are asleep.'	The centurion says that the prisoners are asleep.
'Lupus in vīllā rūsticā habitat.'	audiō **Lupum** in vīllā rūsticā **habitāre**.
'Lupus is living in his country villa.'	I hear that Lupus is living in his country villa.

4 Further examples of direct and indirect statements:

1 'hostēs appropinquant.'
2 nūntius dīcit hostēs appropinquāre.
3 dominus crēdit fugitīvōs in fossā latēre. *(ie hidden)*
4 'Agricola bellum in Calēdoniā gerit.' → *wear or achieve*
5 audiō Agricolam bellum in Calēdoniā gerere.
6 rhētor putat fīlium meum dīligenter labōrāre.

Country villas

Many wealthy Romans, like Lupus on pages 3–9, owned both a town house in Rome and at least one villa in the country. There they could escape from the noise and heat of the city, especially during the unhealthy months of late summer, and relax from the pressures of private business and public duties.

Some of these country houses were fairly close to Rome; their owners could get a day's work done in the city and then travel out to their villa before nightfall. The villas were generally either on the coast, like Pliny's villa at Laurentum, or on the hills around Rome, for example at Tibur, where the Emperor Hadrian owned the most spectacular mansion of all, surrounded by specially constructed imitations of buildings that had impressed him on his travels.

But other country villas were further afield. A popular area was Campania; the coastline of the bay of Naples was dotted with the villas of wealthy men, while holiday resorts such as Baiae enjoyed a reputation for fast living and dubious morals.

Country villas naturally varied in design, but they usually contained some or all of the following features: a series of dining and reception rooms for entertaining guests, often giving extensive views of the surrounding countryside; a set of baths, heated by hypocausts, containing the full range of apodyterium, tepidarium, caldarium and frigidarium; long colonnades where the owner and his friends might walk, or even ride, sheltered from the rain or from the direct heat of the sun; and extensive parkland, farmland or gardens, preferably with plenty of shade and running water. In a corner of the estate there might be a small shrine, dedicated to the protecting gods.

Pliny's letters include descriptions of two of his villas; the descriptions are detailed without always being clear, and many scholars have tried to reconstruct the plans of the villas, without reaching agreement. An attempt at the plan of Pliny's Laurentine villa is shown below, together with a model based on the

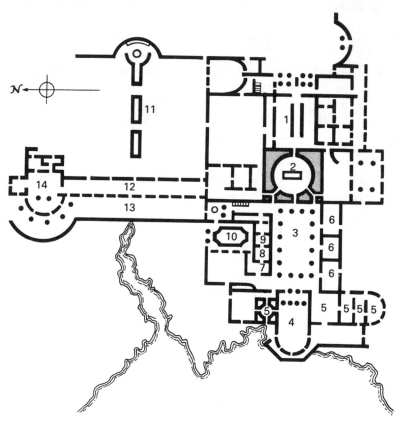

1 Atrium	6 Slaves' rooms	11 Ornamental garden with
2 Courtyard	7 Tepidarium	vine pergola
3 Inner courtyard	8 Apodyterium	12 Covered colonnade
4 Dining-room	9 Caldarium	13 Terrace
5 Bedrooms	10 Heated swimming-bath	14 Pliny's private suite

Model of Pliny's villa at Laurentum

plan. Among the villa's special features were the heated swimming-bath (10), the big semi-circular recess at the end of the chief dining-room (4), designed to provide the dinner-guests with an impressive panorama of the sea, and the covered colonnade (12) leading to Pliny's private suite (14). This suite was Pliny's own addition to the building, and it provided him with quiet and privacy; for example, at the noisy mid-winter festival of the Saturnalia, Pliny could retire to his suite while his slaves enjoyed themselves in the main villa, so that he did not get in the way of their celebrations and they did not disturb his peace.

One of the most popular recreations for a wealthy Roman on his country estate was hunting. Hares, deer or wild boars were tracked down and then pursued into nets where they could be speared to death. Long ropes, to which brightly-coloured feathers were attached, were slung from trees to cut off the animal's retreat and frighten it back towards the nets. The actual chasing was often left to slaves and dogs, while the hunter contented himself with waiting at the nets and spearing the boar or deer when it had become thoroughly entangled. Pliny, for example, in reporting a successful

15

expedition on which he caught three boars, says that he took his stilus and writing-tablets with him to the hunt and jotted ideas down under the inspiration of the woodland scene while he waited for the boars to appear. But although Pliny's description of hunting

Picnic during a hunt, from a mosaic

is a very peaceful one, the sport still had its dangers: a cornered boar might turn on its pursuers, and a hunter who was slow with his spear might be gashed nastily and even fatally.

Fishing was also popular, and could easily be combined with rowing or sailing, either on the sea (in the bay of Naples, for example) or on such lakes as the Lucrine lake, famous for its fish and its oysters. A lazier method of fishing is described by Martial, who refers to a villa with a bedroom directly overlooking the sea, so that the occupant could drop a fishing-line from the window and catch a fish without even getting out of bed.

Some of Pliny's letters describe his daily routine at his country villas. He spent most of his time in gentle exercise (walking, riding or occasionally hunting), working on a speech or other piece of writing, dealing with his tenant-farmers (colōnī), entertaining friends, dining, or listening to a reading or music. He often spent part of the afternoon reading a Greek or Latin speech aloud 'for the sake of both voice and digestion'. (Pliny often spoke publicly in the law courts and the senate, and he was naturally anxious to keep his voice in good trim.)

But a country villa of this kind was not just for holiday relaxation; it was an important investment. Often there was a farm attached to the house, and the property would usually include an extensive area of land which the owner might farm himself or lease to tenant-farmers. In the ancient world, by far the commonest way of investing money was to buy land. It is not surprising that many of Pliny's letters deal with the day-to-day problems of land management. He agonises over whether to buy a neighbouring piece of land, fertile and conveniently situated but long neglected; he asks the emperor to excuse him from Rome so that he can be on one of his estates at a time when the tenancy is changing hands; and when his tenants get into difficulties and are heavily in debt, he works out a system for converting their rent from a cash sum into a proportion of their crop. He likes to present himself as an ignorant amateur with no interest in the running of his villas, but some of his comments give the impression that he was in fact enthusiastic, practical and shrewd. He was also very successful; one of his villas alone brought him an income of 400,000 sesterces a year.

Vocabulary checklist

ager, agrī – field
an – or
   utrum . . . an – whether . . . or
caveō, cavēre, cāvī – beware
cūrae esse – be a matter of concern
ideō – for this reason
   ideō . . . quod – for the reason that, because
inde – then
īnsum, inesse, īnfuī – be in, be inside
magis – more
male – badly, unfavourably
mentior, mentīrī, mentītus sum – lie, tell a lie
meritus, merita, meritum – deserved, well-deserved
moror, morārī, morātus sum – delay
officium, officiī – duty
puto, putāre, putāvī – think
quandō? – when?
quidem – indeed
quotiēns – whenever
rēctē – rightly, properly
relēgō, relēgāre, relēgāvī, relēgātus – exile
rūs, rūris – country, countryside
simul – at the same time
supplicium, suppliciī – punishment, penalty
vīcīnus, vīcīnī – neighbour
virgō, virginis – virgin

recitātiō

Marcus Valerius Mārtiālis

I

in audītōriō exspectant multī cīvēs. adsunt ut Valerium Mārtiālem, poētam
nōtissimum, recitantem audiant. omnēs inter sē colloquuntur. subitō signum
datur ut taceant; audītōrium intrat poēta ipse. audītōribus plaudentibus,
Mārtiālis scaenam ascendit ut versūs suōs recitet.

5 Mārtiālis: salvēte, amīcī. (*librum ēvolvit.*) prīmum recitāre volō
               versūs quōsdam nūper dē Sabidiō compositōs.

complūrēs audītōrēs sē convertunt ut Sabidium, quī in ultimō sellārum ōrdine
sedet, spectent.

     Mārtiālis: nōn amo tē, Sabidī, nec possum dīcere quārē.
10   hoc tantum possum dīcere – nōn amo tē.

     audītor: (*cum amīcīs susurrāns*) illōs versūs nōn intellegō. cūr poēta
              dīcere nōn potest quārē Sabidium nōn amet?
     prīmus amīcus: (*susurrāns*) scīlicet poēta ipse causam nescit.
     secundus amīcus: (*susurrāns*) immō, poēta optimē scit quārē
15   Sabidium nōn amet: sed tam foeda et obscēna est causa
               ut poēta eam patefacere nōlit.
     aliī audītōrēs: st! st!
     prīmus amīcus: hem! audītōrēs nōbīs imperant ut taceāmus.
     Mārtiālis: nunc de Laecāniā et Thāide, fēminīs 'nōtissimīs':
20   (*audītōrēs sibi rīdent.*)

            Thāis habet <u>nigrōs</u>, niveōs Laecānia <u>dentēs</u>.*
            quae ratiō est? . . .
     audītor: (*interpellāns*)   . . . ēmptōs haec habet, illa suōs!

Mārtiālis, interpellātiōne valdē īrātus, dē scaenā dēscendit ut audītōrem
25 *vituperet.*
     Mārtiālis: ego poēta sum, tū tantum audītor. ego hūc invītātus sum
               ut recitem, tū ut audiās. (*subitō audītōrem agnōscit.*) hem!

---

*Some noun-and-adjective phrases, in which an adjective is separated by one
word or more from the noun which it describes, have been underlined.

Mārtiālis, interpellātiōne valdē īrātus, dē scaenā dēscendit ut audītōrem vituperet. (lines 24—5)

scio quis sīs. tū Pontiliānus es, quī semper mē rogās ut
libellōs meōs tibi mittam. at nunc, mī Pontiliāne, tibi
dīcere possum quārē semper mittere recūsem. (*ad* 30
scaenam reversus, recitātiōnem renovat.)

cūr nōn mitto meōs tibi, Pontiliāne, libellōs?
nē mihi tū mittās, Pontiliāne, tuōs!

omnēs praeter Pontiliānum rīdent. Pontiliānus autem tam īrātus est ut ē sellā
surgat. ad scaenam sē praecipitāre cōnātur ut Mārtiālem pulset, sed amīcī eum 35
retinent.

audītōriō: audītōrium *auditorium, hall*
  (used for public readings)
colloquuntur: colloquī *talk, chat*
audītōribus: audītor *listener, (pl.) audience*
ēvolvit: ēvolvere *unroll, open*
complūrēs *several*
obscēna: obscēnus *obscene, disgusting*
st! *hush!*

Thāide *ablative of* Thāis
quae?: quī? *what?*
ratiō *reason*
haec . . . illa *this one (Laecania)*
  . . . that one (Thais)
interpellātiōne: interpellātiō *interruption*
renovat: renovāre *continue, resume*

II

Mārtiālis, quī iam ūnam hōram recitat, ad fīnem librī appropinquat.

Mārtiālis: amīcī meī dīcunt poētam quendam, Fīdentīnum
nōmine, mcōs libellōs quasi suōs recitāre. nunc igitur
Fīdentīnō hoc dīcere volō:

5   quem recitās <u>meus</u> est, ō Fīdentīne, <u>libellus</u>.
        sed male cum recitās, incipit esse tuus.

complūrēs audītōrēs, Fīdentīnī amīcī, sibilant; cēterī rīdent.

Mārtiālis: postrēmō pauca dē prīncipe nostrō, Domitiānō Augustō, dīcere velim. aliquōs versūs nūper dē illā aulā
10   ingentī composuī quae in monte Palātīnō stat:

        aethera contingit <u>nova</u> nostrī prīncipis <u>aula</u>;
        clārius in <u>tōtō</u> sōl videt <u>orbe</u> nihil.
        <u>haec</u>, Auguste, tamen, quae vertice sīdera pulsat,
        pār <u>domus</u> est caelō sed minor est dominō.

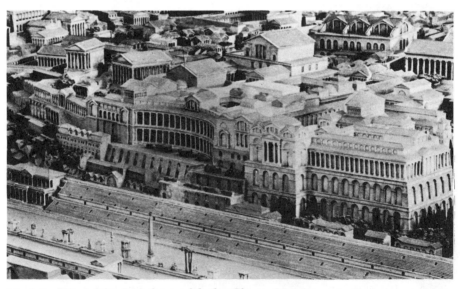

Model of Domitian's palace with the Circus Maximus in front

plērīque   audītōrēs   vehementissimē   plaudunt;   animadvertunt   enim 15
Epaphrodītum, Domitiānī lībertum, in audītōriō adesse. ūnus audītor tamen,
M'. Acīlius Glabriō, tālī adulātiōne offēnsus, nōn modo plausū abstinet sed ē
sellā surgit et ex audītōriō exit. quā audāciā attonitus, Mārtiālis paulīsper
immōtus stat; deinde ad extrēmam scaenam prōcēdit ut plausum excipiat. ūnus
tamen audītor exclāmat: 20

audītor: sed quid dē mē, Mārtiālis? epigramma dē mē
            compōnere nunc potes?
Mārtiālis: dē tē, homuncule? quis es et quālis?
audītor: nōmine Diaulus sum. artem medicīnae nūper ex-
            ercēbam . . . 25
alius audītor: . . . at nunc vespillō es!
(*omnēs rīdent; rīdet praesertim Mārtiālis.*)
Mārtiālis: bene! nunc epigramma accipe, mī Diaule:

>   nūper erat medicus, nunc est vespillo Diaulus.
>   quod vespillo facit, fēcerat et medicus. 30

cachinnant multī; ērubēscit Diaulus. Mārtiālis, recitātiōne ita perfectā, ex
audītōriō ēgreditur, omnibus praeter Diaulum plaudentibus. servī ingressī
audītōribus vīnum cibumque offerunt.

sibilant: sibilāre *hiss*
prīncipe: prīnceps *emperor*
composuī: compōnere *compose, make up*
monte Palātīnō: mōns Palātīnus *the Palatine hill*
aethera *accusative of* aethēr *sky, heaven*
contingit: contingere *touch*
clārius . . . nihil *nothing more splendid*
orbe: orbis *globe, world*
vertice: vertex *top, peak*
sīdera: sīdus *star*
pār *equal*
minor . . . dominō *smaller than its master*
M'. = Mānius
adulātiōne: adulātiō *flattery*
ad extrēmam scaenam *to the edge of the stage*
vespillō *undertaker*
quod = id quod *what*
et = etiam *also*

Language note

1 In Unit IIIA, you met the *imperfect* and *pluperfect* tenses of the subjunctive:

imperfect
haruspex aderat ut victimam **īnspiceret**.
The soothsayer was there in order that he might examine the victim.
    or, in more natural English:
The soothsayer was there to examine the victim.

pluperfect
rēx prīncipēs rogāvit num discordiam **composuissent**.
The king asked the chieftains whether they had settled their quarrel.

2 In Stage 36, you have met sentences like these:

cīvēs conveniunt ut poētam **audiant**.
The citizens are gathering in order that they may hear the poet.
    or, in more natural English:
The citizens are gathering to hear the poet.

Mārtiālis dīcere nōn potest quārē Sabidium nōn **amet**.
Martial is unable to say why he does not like Sabidius.

The form of the verb in heavy print is the *present* tense of the subjunctive.

3 Further examples:
    I want to find out which
 1 cognōscere volō quid illī fabrī aedificent.   *~~~~*
 2 tam saevus est dominus noster ut servōs pūnīre numquam
    dēsinat.
    I work everyday in the field
 3 in agrīs cotīdiē labōrō ut cibum līberīs meīs praebeam.
 4 nōn intellegimus quārē dēspērētis.

why

4 Compare the present subjunctive with the present indicative:

	present indicative (3rd person singular and plural)	*present subjunctive (3rd person singular and plural)*
first conjugation	portat	portet
	portant	portent
second conjugation	docet	doceat
	docent	doceant
third conjugation	trahit	trahat
	trahunt	trahant
fourth conjugation	audit	audiat
	audiunt	audiant

The present subjunctive of all four conjugations is set out in full on p.140 of the Language Information section.

5 For the present subjunctive of irregular verbs, see p.145.

epigrammata Mārtiālia

The following epigrams, and also the ones which appeared on pages 20–3, were written by Marcus Valerius Martialis (Martial) and published between A.D. 86 and 101.

I   *dē Tuccā, quī Mārtiālem saepe ōrat ut libellōs sibi dōnet*

    exigis ut <u>nostrōs</u> dōnem tibi, Tucca, <u>libellōs</u>.
       nōn faciam: nam vīs vēndere, nōn legere.

    dōnet: dōnāre *give*   exigis: exigere *demand*   nostrōs: noster = meus *my*

    Why does Martial refuse Tucca's request?

II   *dē Sextō, iuvene glōriōsō*

    dīcis amōre tuī <u>bellās</u> ardēre <u>puellās</u>,
       quī faciem sub aquā, Sexte, natantis habēs.

    glōriōsō: glōriōsus *boastful*   bellās: bellus *pretty*   faciem: faciēs *face*

    Judging from Martial's description, what impression do you have of Sextus' appearance?

III   *dē Symmachō medicō discipulīsque eius centum*

    languēbam: sed tū comitātus prōtinus ad mē
       vēnistī <u>centum</u>, Symmache, <u>discipulīs</u>.
    centum mē tetigēre <u>manūs</u> Aquilōne <u>gelātae</u>;
       nōn habuī febrem, Symmache: nunc habeō.

    discipulīs: discipulus *pupil, student*   Aquilōne: Aquilō *North wind*
    languēbam: languēre *feel weak, feel sick*   gelātae: gelāre *freeze*
    prōtinus *immediately*   febrem: febris *fever*
    tetigēre = tetigērunt: tangere *touch*

    Why do you think Martial repeats the word 'centum' (lines 2–3) and uses the phrase 'Aquilōne gelātae' (line 3)?

IV   *dē Catullō, quī saepe dīcit Mārtiālem hērēdem sibi esse*

hērēdem tibi mē, Catulle, dīcis.
nōn crēdam nisi lēgerō, Catulle.

When will Martial believe Catullus' promise? Why do you
think he will believe it then, but not believe it earlier?

V   *dē Quīntō, quī Thāida lūscam amat*

'Thāida Quīntus amat.' 'quam Thāida?' 'Thāida lūscam.'
    ūnum oculum Thāis nōn habet, ille duōs.

Thāida *accusative of* Thāis
lūscam: lūscus *one-eyed*
quam?: quī? *which?*

What do the last two words suggest about (a) Quintus,
(b) Thais?

'**centum mē tetigēre manūs Aquilōne gelātae.**' (III, line 3)

VI *dē Vacerrā, quī veterēs poētās sōlōs mīrātur*

> mīrāris <u>veterēs</u>, Vacerra, sōlōs
> nec laudās nisi mortuōs <u>poētās</u>.
> ignōscās petimus, Vacerra: tantī
> nōn est, ut placeam tibī, perīre.

mīrātur: mīrārī *admire*
ignōscās petimus = petimus ut nōbīs ignōscās
tantī nōn est . . . perīre *it is not worth dying*

Do people like Vacerra still exist nowadays?

Language note

1 From Stage 3 onwards, you have met phrases in which an adjective is placed next to the noun it describes:

ad **silvam obscūram**	to the dark wood
contrā **multōs hostēs**	against many enemies
in **magnā nāve**	in a big ship

2 In Unit IIIA, you met phrases in which an adjective is separated by a preposition from the noun which it describes:

tōtam per **urbem**	through the whole city
omnibus cum **mīlitibus**	with all the soldiers
hōc ex **oppidō**	from this town

3 In Stage 36, you have met sentences like these:

cūr nōn mitto **meōs** tibi, Pontiliāne, **libellōs**?
Why do I not send you my writings, Pontilianus?

aethera contingit **nova** nostrī prīncipis **aula**.
The new palace of our emperor touches the sky.

This kind of word order, in which an adjective is separated by one or more words from the noun which it describes, is particularly common in verse.

Further examples:

1 dēnique centuriō **magnam** pervēnit ad **urbem**.
2 nox erat, et **caelō** fulgēbat lūna **serēnō**. (*from a poem by Horace*)
3 flūminis in rīpā nunc **noster** dormit **amīcus**.

4 In each of the following examples, pick out the Latin adjective and say which noun it is describing:

1 atque iterum ad Trōiam magnus mittētur Achillēs. (*Virgil*)
   And great Achilles will be sent again to Troy.
2 ergō sollicitae tū causa, pecūnia, vītae! (*Propertius*)
   Therefore you, money, are the cause of an anxious life!
3 rōbustus quoque iam taurīs iuga solvet arātor. (*Virgil*)
   Now, too, the strong ploughman will unfasten the yoke from the bulls.

5 Translate the following examples:

1 *On a journey*
   cōnspicimus montēs atque altae moenia Rōmae.
2 *Cries of pain*
   clāmōrēs simul horrendōs ad sīdera tollit. (*Virgil*)
3 *A foreigner*
   hic posuit nostrā nūper in urbe pedem. (*Propertius*)
4 *Preparations for battle*
   tum iuvenis validā sustulit arma manū.
5 *The foolishness of sea travel*
   cūr cupiunt nautae saevās properāre per undās?

moenia *city walls*
horrendōs : horrendus *horrifying*
properāre *hurry*

Pick out the adjective in each example and say which noun it is describing.

Exercises

1 Study the form and meaning of the following nouns and adjectives and give the meaning of the untranslated words:

ōtium	leisure, idleness	ōtiōsus	idle, on holiday
spatium	space	spatiōsus	spacious, large
fōrma	beauty	fōrmōsus	
līmus	mud	līmōsus	
herba		herbōsus	grassy
bellum		bellicōsus	aggressive, warlike
pretium	price, value	pretiōsus	
perīculum		perīculōsus	
fūror	madness, rage	fūriōsus	
damnum		damnōsus	harmful, damaging

Match each of the following Latin adjectives with the correct English translation:

Latin: fūmōsus, iocōsus, ventōsus, perfidiōsus, annōsus
English: treacherous, smoky, fond of jokes, old, blown by the winds

2 Complete each sentence with the right word and then translate.

1 Mārtiālis versum dē Imperātōre compōnere . . . . . . (cōnābātur, ēgrediēbātur)

2 Glabriō amīcum . . . . . ut ad urbem revenīret. (cōnspicābātur, hortābātur)

3 mīlitēs ducem ad ultimās regiōnēs Britanniae . . . . . . (sequēbantur, suspicābantur)

4 omnēs senātōrēs dē victōriā Agricolae . . . . . . (adipīscēbantur, loquēbantur)

5 pauper, quī multōs cāsūs . . . . ., nihilōminus contentus erat. (patiēbātur, precābātur)

6 clientēs, quī patrōnum ad forum . . . . ., viam complēbant. (comitābantur, proficīscēbantur)

3 Translate each sentence; then, with the help of the tables on pages 126–34 and 144 of the Language Information section, change the words in heavy print from singular to plural, and translate again.

1 tribūnus **centuriōnem callidum** laudāvit.
2 frāter meus, postquam **hoc templum** vīdit, obstupefactus est.
3 senex **amīcō dēspērantī** auxilium tulit.
4 ubi **est puella**? **eam** salūtāre volō.
5 iuvenis, **hastā ingentī** armātus, ad vēnātiōnem contendit.
6 **puer**, **quem** herī pūnīvī, hodiē labōrāre nōn **potest**.

4 Complete each sentence with the most suitable verb from the list below, using the correct form, and then translate. Do not use any verb more than once.

exstīnxit	accēpit	iussit	recitāvit	dūxit
exstīnxērunt	accēpērunt	iussērunt	recitāvērunt	dūxērunt
exstīnctus est	acceptus est	iussus est	recitātus est	ductus est
exstīnctī sunt	acceptī sunt	iussī sunt	recitātī sunt	ductī sunt

1 ignis tandem ā mīlitibus . . . . . .
2 poēta multōs versūs dē Imperātōre . . . . . .
3 captīvī per viās urbis in triumphō . . . . . .
4 clientēs pecūniam laetissimē . . . . . .
5 lībertus ad aulam contendere . . . . . .

Recitationes

The easiest and commonest way for a Roman author to bring his work to the notice of the public was to read it aloud to them. For example, a poet might choose a convenient spot, such as a street corner, a barber's shop, or a colonnade in the forum, and recite his poems to anyone who cared to stop and listen. Like any kind of street performance or sales-talk, this could be very entertaining or very annoying for the passers-by. In an exaggerated but colourful complaint, Martial claims that a poet called Ligurinus used to recite continually at him, whether he was eating dinner, hurrying along the street, swimming in the baths, or using the public lavatories, and that even when he went to sleep, Ligurinus woke him up and began reciting again.

Often, however, a writer's work received its first reading in a more comfortable place than the street corner, with a carefully chosen group of listeners rather than a casual collection of passers-by. A natural audience for a writer was his patron, if he had one, and his patron's family and friends. For example, Virgil read sections of his poem the *Aeneid* to the Emperor Augustus and to Augustus' sister Octavia, who is said to have fainted when Virgil reached a part of the poem which referred to her dead son Marcellus. A writer might also invite friends to his house and read his work to them there, perhaps inviting them to make comments or criticisms before he composed a final version of the work. This kind of reading sometimes took place at a dinner-party. If the host was an accomplished and entertaining writer, this would add to the guests' enjoyment of the meal; but some hosts made great nuisances of themselves by reading boring or feeble work to their dinner-guests.

The public reading of a writer's work often took place at a special occasion known as a 'recitātiō', like the one on pages 20–3, in which an invited audience had a chance to hear the author's work and could decide whether or not to buy a copy or have a copy made. The recitatio might be given at the writer's house, or more often the

Clay figure of an elderly man reading

house of his patron; or a hall (audītōrium) might be specially hired for the purpose. Invitations were sent out. Cushioned chairs were set out at the front for the more distinguished guests; benches were placed behind them, and, if the recitatio was a very grand occasion, tiered seats on temporary scaffolding. Slaves gave out programmes to the audience as they arrived, and if the writer was unscrupulous or over-anxious, one or two friends might be stationed at particular points in the audience with instructions to applaud at the right moments.

When all was ready, the reading started. Generally the author himself read his work, though there were exceptions. (Pliny, for example, knew that he was bad at reading poetry; so although he read his speeches himself, he had his poems read by a freedman.) The writer, specially dressed for the occasion in a freshly laundered toga, stepped forward and delivered a short introduction (praefātiō) to his work, then sat to read the work itself. The recital might be continued on a second and third day, sometimes at the request of the audience.

Things did not always go smoothly at recitationes. The Emperor Claudius, when young, embarked on a series of readings from his own historical work, but disaster struck when an enormously fat man joined the audience and sat down on a flimsy bench, which collapsed beneath him; in the general mirth it became impossible for the reading to continue. Pliny records a more serious incident during the reign of Trajan. A historian, who had announced that he would continue his reading in a few days' time, was approached by a group of people who begged him not to read the next instalment because they knew it would be dealing with some fairly recent events in which they had been concerned, and which they did not want read out in public. It is possible that the author concerned was the historian Tacitus, describing the past misdeeds of the Emperor Domitian and his associates. The historian granted the request and cancelled the next instalment of the reading. However, as Pliny pointed out, cancelling the recitatio did not mean that the men's misdeeds would stay unknown: people would be all the more curious to read the history, in order to find out why the recitatio had been cancelled.

Pliny, who gave recitationes of his own work and also regularly

Relief showing a Roman reading from a book

attended those of other people, was very shocked at the frivolous way in which some members of the audience behaved: 'Some of them loiter and linger outside the hall, and send their slaves in to find out how far the recitatio has got; then, when the slaves report that the author has nearly finished his reading, they come in at last – and even then they don't always stay, but slip out before the end, some of them sheepishly and furtively, others boldly and brazenly.'

Some Roman writers are very critical of recitationes. Seneca, for example, says that when the author says to the audience 'Shall I read some more?' they usually reply 'Yes, please do', but privately they are praying for the man to be struck dumb. Juvenal sarcastically includes recitationes among the dangers and disadvantages of life in Rome, together with fires and falling buildings. In fact, the work read out must have varied enormously in quality: occasional masterpieces, a sprinkling of good-to-middling work and plenty of rubbish. A more serious criticism of recitationes is that they encouraged writers to think too much about impressing their audience. One author admitted: 'Much of what I say is said not because it pleases me but because it will please my hearers.'

However, in first-century Rome, when every copy of a book had to be produced individually by hand, recitationes filled a real need. They enabled the author to bring his work to the notice of many people without the expense and labour of creating large numbers of copies. Recitationes were also useful from the audience's point of view. It was far harder in Roman than in modern times to go into a bookshop, run one's eye over the titles and covers, sample the contents of a few likely-looking books, and make one's choice. The physical nature of a Roman book (see illustration opposite) meant that there was no such thing as a cover; the title was printed not on a convenient part of the book but on a label attached to it, which was often lost; and the act of unrolling and reading a book, then rerolling it ready for the next reader, was so laborious that sampling and browsing were virtually impossible. The recitatio allowed the author to present his work to an audience conveniently, economically and (if he were a good reader) attractively.

Vocabulary checklist

animadvertō, animadvertere, animadvertī, animadversus – notice,
    take notice of
arma, armōrum – arms, weapons
causa, causae – reason, cause
discipulus, discipulī – pupil, student
dōnō, dōnāre, dōnāvī, dōnātus – give
extrēmus, extrēma, extrēmum – furthest
fīnis, fīnis – end
ignis, ignis – fire
mīror, mīrārī, mīrātus sum – admire, wonder at
nē – that . . . not, in order that . . . not
niger, nigra, nigrum – black
offendō, offendere, offendī, offēnsus – displease, offend
pār, *gen.* paris – equal
plērīque, plēraeque, plēraque – most, the majority
praesēns, *gen.* praesentis – present, ready
praesertim – especially
praeter – except
recitō, recitāre, recitāvī, recitātus – recite, read out
regiō, regiōnis – region
tangō, tangere, tetigī, tāctus – touch
vacuus, vacua, vacuum – empty
vetus, *gen.* veteris – old

cōnsilium

Agricola, Calēdoniīs victīs, epistulam nūntiō dictat. in hāc epistulā Agricola victōriam Rōmānōrum Imperātōrī nūntiat.

Agricola dīcit exercitum Rōmānum Calēdoniōs superāvisse.

Agricola dīcit multōs hostēs periisse, paucōs effūgisse.

'aliae gentēs nūntiōs iam mīsērunt quī pācem petant.'

Agricola dīcit aliās gentēs nūntiōs mīsisse quī pācem petant.

epistula

Cn. Iūlius Agricola Domitiānō Imperātōrī salūtem dīcit.
septimus annus est, domine, ex quō pater tuus, dīvus Vespasiānus,
ad prōvinciam Britanniam mē mīsit, ut barbarōs superārem. tū
ipse, audītīs precibus meīs, iussistī Calēdoniōs quoque in populī
5 Rōmānī potestātem redigī. nunc tibi nūntiō exercitum Rōmānum
magnam victōriam rettulisse. bellum est cōnfectum; Calēdoniī sunt
victī.

   initiō huius aestātis, exercitus noster ad ultimās partēs Britanniae
pervēnit. hostēs, adventū nostrō cognitō, prope montem Graupium
10 sē ad proelium īnstrūxērunt. ibi mīlitēs nostrī, spē glōriae adductī,
victōriam nōmine tuō dignam rettulērunt. nōn satis cōnstat quot
hostēs perierint; sciō tamen paucissimōs effūgisse. explōrātōrēs meī
affirmant nōnnūllōs superstitēs, salūte dēspērātā, etiam casās suās
incendisse atque coniugēs līberōsque manū suā occīdisse.
15   dē bellō satis dīxī. nunc bellōrum causae tollendae sunt; nunc pāx
firmanda est. omnibus eīs pepercī quī sē dēdidērunt. per tōtam
prōvinciam centuriōnēs frūmentum ac tribūtum mollius exigere
iussī sunt. ego ipse Britannōs hortātus sum ut templa, fora, domōs

exstruant; filiīs prīncipum persuāsī ut linguam Latīnam discant.
mōrēs Rōmānī ā Britannīs iam adsūmuntur; ubīque aspiciuntur 20
togae.

ūna cūra tamen mē sollicitat. timeō nē inquiēta sit Britannia,
dum Hibernia īnsula in lībertāte manet. quod sī Hibernōs
superāverimus, nōn modo pācem in Britanniā habēbimus, sed
etiam magnās dīvitiās comparābimus; audiō enim ex mercātōribus 25
metalla Hiberniae aurum multum continēre. equidem crēdō hanc
īnsulam legiōne ūnā obtinērī posse. mīlitēs sunt parātī; signum
Imperātōris alacriter exspectātur. valē.

Cn. = Gnaeus
in . . . potestātem redigī: in potestātem redigere *bring under the control*
victōriam rettulisse: victōriam referre *win a victory*
initiō: initium *beginning*
aestātis: aestās *summer*
proelium *battle*
satis cōnstat *it is generally agreed*
affirmant: affirmāre *declare*
coniugēs: coniūnx *wife*
tollendae sunt: tollere *remove, do away with*
firmanda est: firmāre *strengthen, establish*
pepercī: parcere *spare*
sē dēdidērunt: sē dēdere *surrender, give oneself up*
tribūtum *tribute, tax*
mollius: molliter *gently, leniently*
adsūmuntur: adsūmere *adopt*
sollicitat: sollicitāre *worry*
timeō nē *I am afraid that*
inquiēta: inquiētus *unsettled*
Hibernia *Ireland*
quod sī *but if*
aurum *gold*
equidem *I indeed*
obtinērī: obtinēre *hold*

When you have read this, answer the questions at the end.

amīcī prīncipis

diē illūcēscente, complūrēs senātōrēs in aulam Domitiānī conveniēbant. nam Domitiānus cōnsilium suum ad aulam arcessī iusserat. senātōrēs, dum Imperātōrem exspectant, anxiī inter sē colloquēbantur. in angulō ātriī L. Catullus Messālīnus, vir
5 maximae auctōritātis, cum Q. Vibiō Crispō, senātōre septuāgintā annōs nātō, susurrābat.

Messālīnus: cūr adeō perturbāris, mī Crispe? nōn intellegō quārē anxius sīs.

Crispus: nōn sine causā perturbor. ego enim prīmus ā
10 Domitiānō sententiam rogābor, quia cōnsulāris sum nātū maximus. at nisi sciam quārē Domitiānus nōs cōnsulere velit, sententiam bene meditātam prō-pōnere nōn poterō.

Messālīnus: difficile est mihi tē adiuvāre, mī amīce. nescio enim
15 quārē Domitiānus nōs arcessīverit. aliī dīcunt nūntium ē Britanniā advēnisse; aliī putant Germānōs rebellāvisse; aliī crēdunt ministrōs Epaphrodītī coniūrātiōnem dēprehendisse. nōn tamen tibi tim-endum est; tū enim es senātor summae auctōritātis.

Crispus: id quod dīcis fortasse vērum est. nihilōminus mihi 20
               semper difficile est intellegere quāle respōnsum
               Domitiānus cupiat. sēnsūs enim vērōs dissimulāre
               solet. sī tamen tū mē adiūveris, sēcūrus erō. vīsne,
               quicquid dīxerō, sententiam similem prōpōnere?
Messālīnus: minimē! perīculum mihi ipsī facere haudquāquam 25
               volō. nihil dīcam priusquam Epaphrodītī sententiam
               audīverō.
Crispus: sed –
Messālīnus: tacē, mī amīce! adest Imperātor.

Q. = Quīntus
cōnsulāris *ex-consul*
meditātam: meditārī *consider*
dēprehendisse: dēprehendere *discover*
sēnsūs: sēnsus *feeling*
quicquid *whatever*
similem: similis *similar*

1 At what time of day does this conversation take place?
2 In lines 4–6, find two words or phrases which suggest that
   Crispus and Messalinus are anxious not to be overheard.
3 Why is Crispus agitated?
4 What three guesses have been made about Domitian's reason for
   calling this meeting?
5 What favour does Crispus ask from Messalinus? Is his request
   granted?
6 By what tactics does Messalinus hope to keep out of trouble at the
   meeting?

Language note

1 Compare the following direct and indirect statements:

direct statements	*indirect statements*
'servus fūgit.'	dominus crēdit servum **fūgisse**.
'The slave has fled.'	The master believes the slave to have fled.
	or, in more natural English: The master believes that the slave has fled.
'Rōmānī multa oppida dēlēvērunt.'	audiō Rōmānōs multa oppida **dēlēvisse**.
'The Romans have destroyed many towns.'	I hear that the Romans have destroyed many towns.

The form of the verb in heavy print is known as the *perfect active infinitive*.

2 Further examples:

1 scio servōs cēnam splendidam parāvisse.
2 'Rōmānī magnam victōriam rettulērunt.'
3 in hāc epistulā Agricola nūntiat Rōmānōs magnam victōriam rettulisse.
4 clientēs putant patrōnum ex urbe discessisse.
5 'hostēs castra in rīpā flūminis posuērunt.'
6 centuriō dīcit hostēs castra in rīpā flūminis posuisse.

3 Compare the perfect active infinitive with the perfect active indicative:

perfect active indicative *(1st person singular)*		*perfect active infinitive*	
portāvī	I have carried	portāvisse	to have carried
docuī	I have taught	docuisse	to have taught
trāxī	I have dragged	trāxisse	to have dragged
audīvī	I have heard	audīvisse	to have heard

cōnsilium Domitiānī

I

dum senātōrēs anxiī inter sē colloquuntur,
ingressus est Domitiānus vultū ita
compositō ut nēmō intellegere posset
utrum īrātus an laetus esset. cum
sequēbatur Epaphrodītus, epistulam manū 5
tenēns.

Domitiānus, ā senātōribus salūtātus,
'nūntius', inquit, 'nōbīs epistulam modo
attulit, ā Cn. Iūliō Agricolā missam. in hāc
epistulā Agricola nūntiat exercitum 10
Rōmānum ad ultimās partēs Britanniae
pervēnisse et magnam victōriam rettulisse.
Epaphrodīte, epistulam recitā.'

epistulā recitātā, Domitiānus, ad Crispum statim conversus,

'quid', inquit, 'dē hāc Agricolae epistulā putās? quid mihi 15
suādēs?'

Crispus diū tacēbat; superciliīs contractīs quasi
rem cōgitāret, oculōs humī dēfīxit. dēnique:

'moderātiōnem', inquit, 'suādeō.'

Domitiānus 'breviter', inquit, 'et commodē 20
locūtus es. tua tamen sententia amplius est
explicanda.'

modo *just now*
suādēs: suādēre *advise, suggest*
superciliīs contractīs: supercilia contrahere *draw eyebrows together, frown*
moderātiōnem: moderātiō *moderation, caution*
breviter *briefly*
commodē *appropriately*
amplius *more fully*

priusquam Crispus respondēret, A. Fabricius Vēientō, cēterīs
paulō audācior, interpellāvit. veritus tamen nē Domitiānum
25 offenderet, verbīs cōnsīderātīs ūsus est:

    'cognōvimus, domine, Cn. Iūlium Agricolam
Calēdoniōs tandem superāvisse. ille tamen victōriā
nimis ēlātus est. Agricola crēdit īnsulam Hiberniam
facile occupārī posse; ego autem puto Agricolam
30   longē errāre; Hibernī enim et ferōcēs et validī sunt. sī
cōpiae nostrae trāns mare in Hiberniam ductae
erunt, magnō perīculō obicientur.'

deinde P. Cornēlius Fuscus, praefectus praetōriō:

    'Aulus Fabricius', inquit, 'commodē et sapienter
35   nōs admonuit. mīsit Agricola nōbīs litterās verbō
speciōsās, rē vērā inānēs. iste septem annōs
Britanniae iam praeest. mīsitne tribūtum septem
annōrum ad aerārium? minimē! ipse in suā epistulā
dīcit centuriōnēs iussōs esse tribūtum mollius
40   exigere; addit sē fīliīs prīncipum persuāsisse ut
linguam Latīnam discant. scīlicet Agricola putat sē ad Britanniam
missum esse ut puerōs doceat, nōn ut barbarōs superet! revocandus
est Agricola et pūniendus.'

tum M'. Acīlius Glabriō, hāc sententiā incēnsus,

45   'Cornēlī Fusce', inquit, 'tū sine causā
Agricolam culpās. eī invidēs quod rēs tam
splendidās gessit. equidem valdē gaudeō
Calēdoniōs superātōs esse. sī Hibernia quoque
ab Agricolā victa erit, tōtam Britanniam in
50   potestāte nostrā habēbimus. absurdum est
Agricolam revocāre priusquam Britannōs
omnīnō superet! quis nostrōrum ducum est
melior quam Agricola? quis dignior est triumphō?'

A. = Aulus
veritus: verērī *be afraid, fear*
cōnsīderātīs: cōnsīderātus *careful,*
   well-considered
ūsus est: ūtī *use*
ēlātus *excited, carried away*
cōpiae *forces*

obicientur: obicere *put in the way of, expose to*
praefectus praetōriō *commander of the*
   praetorian guard
sapienter *wisely*
speciōsās: speciōsus *impressive*
aerārium *treasury*

II

cēterī, audāciā Glabriōnis obstupefactī, oculōs in Imperātōrem
dēfīxōs tenēbant nec quicquam dīcere audēbant. ille tamen nec
verbō nec vultū sēnsūs ostendit. deinde Epaphrodītus, ad
Glabriōnem conversus,

'num comparās', inquit, 'hanc inānem 5
Agricolae victōriam cum rēbus splendidīs ab
Imperātōre nostrō gestīs? nōnne audīvistī, mī
Glabriō, Imperātōrem ipsum proximō annō
multa mīlia Germānōrum superāvisse? num
oblītus es prīncipēs Germānōs, catēnīs vīnctōs, 10
per viās urbis in triumphō dēductōs esse?'

tum Messālīnus, simulatque haec Epaphrodītī verba audīvit,
occāsiōne ūsus,

'satis cōnstat', inquit, 'nūllōs hostēs ferōciōrēs
Germānīs esse, nūllum ducem Domitiānō 15
Augustō esse meliōrem. scīmus etiam Agricolam in prōvinciā septem annōs mānsisse.
ipse affirmat tam fidēlēs sibi legiōnēs esse ut ad
Hiberniam sine timōre prōgredī possit.
cavendum est nōbīs! quis nostrum Sulpiciī Galbae exemplum 20
nescit? omnēs meminimus Galbam quoque prōvinciam septem
annōs rēxisse; omnēs scīmus Galbam cupīdine imperiī corruptum
esse; scīmus Galbam dēnique bellum contrā patriam suam gessisse.
num Glabriō cupit Agricolam fierī Imperātōrem? Agricola, meā
sententiā, revocandus, laudandus, tollendus est.' 25

Glabriō nihil respondit. nōn enim dubitābat quīn Imperātōrem
graviter offendisset. Messālīnī sententiam cēterī senātōrēs alacriter
secūtī sunt.

Domitiānus autem nūllum signum dedit neque odiī neque gaudiī
neque invidiae. cōnsiliō tandem dīmissō, in ātriō sōlus mānsit; 30
multa in animō dē Glabriōne atque Agricolā volvēbat.

nec . . . nec *neither . . . nor*	oblītus es: oblīvīscī *forget*	fierī *to become, to be made*
comparās: comparāre	meminimus *we remember*	nōn . . . dubitābat quīn *did*
compare	rēxisse: regere *rule*	*not doubt that*
gestīs: gerere *achieve*	cupīdine: cupīdō *desire*	odiī: odium *hatred*
proximō: proximus *last*	imperiī: imperium *power*	invidiae: invidia *jealousy, envy*

Language note

1 Compare the following direct and indirect statements:

direct statements
'captīvī līberātī sunt.'
'The prisoners have been freed.'

indirect statements
scio captīvōs **līberātōs esse**.
I know the prisoners to have been freed.
   or, in more natural English:
I know that the prisoners have been freed.

'nūntius ab Agricolā missus est.'
'A messenger has been sent by Agricola.'

Domitiānus dīcit nūntium ab Agricolā **missum esse**.
Domitian says that a messenger has been sent by Agricola.

The form of the verb in heavy print is known as the *perfect passive infinitive*.

2 Further examples:

1 'multī Calēdoniī occīsī sunt.'
2 in hāc epistulā Agricola nūntiat multōs Calēdoniōs occīsōs esse.
3 audiō lībertātem omnibus servīs datam esse.
4 nauta crēdit quattuor nāvēs tempestāte dēlētās esse.
5 'templum novum in forō exstrūctum est.'
6 mercātōrēs dīcunt templum novum in forō exstrūctum esse.

3 Compare the perfect passive infinitive with the perfect passive indicative:

perfect passive indicative (1st person singular)		*perfect passive infinitive*	
portātus sum	I have been carried	portātus esse	to have been carried
doctus sum	I have been taught	doctus esse	to have been taught
tractus sum	I have been dragged	tractus esse	to have been dragged
audītus sum	I have been heard	audītus esse	to have been heard

Notice that the perfect passive infinitive contains a participle ('portātus', etc.) which changes its ending in the usual way to agree with the noun it describes:

videō cibum **parātum** esse.   I see that the food has been prepared.

videō victimās **parātās** esse.   I see that the victims have been prepared.

Exercises

1 Complete each sentence with the most suitable word from the list below, and then translate.

audītō, exstruēbātur, prōcēdere, imperātōrī, esset

1 in summō monte novum templum . . . . . .
2 nūntius, simulatque advēnit, ... epistulam trādidit.
3 strepitū . . . . ., cōnsul ē lectō surrēxit.
4 facile cognōvī quis auctor fraudis . . . . . .
5 putō pompam per forum iam . . . . . .

2 In each pair of sentences, translate sentence 'a'; then, with the help of pages 138–9 of the Language Information section, express the same idea by completing the verb in sentence 'b' with a passive form, and translate again.

For example: a   senātōrēs Domitiānum timent.
              b   Domitiānus ā senātōribus timē. . . .
Translated and completed, this becomes:
a   senātōrēs Domitiānum timent.
    The senators fear Domitian.
b   Domitiānus ā senātōribus timētur.
    Domitian is feared by the senators.

1a dux equitēs iam incitat.
1b equitēs ā duce iam incita. . . .
2a exercitus noster oppidum mox dēlēbit.
2b oppidum ab exercitū nostrō mox dēlē. . . .

(continued)

In sentences 3–6, nouns as well as verbs have to be completed. Refer if necessary to the table of nouns on pp.126–7.

3a multī cīvēs lūdōs spectābunt.
3b lūdī ā multīs cīv. . . spectā. . . .
4a puellae ātrium ōrnābant.
4b ātrium ā puell. . . ōrnā. . . .
5a puer victimās ad āram dūcēbat.
5b victimae ad āram ā puer. . . dūcē. . . .
6a mercātor servum accūsābat.
6b serv. . . ā mercātōr. . . accūsā. . . .

3 Translate each sentence into Latin by selecting correctly from the list of Latin words.

1 The enemy have been surrounded by our army.
    hostēs   ad exercitum   nostrō   circumventus est
    hostibus   ab exercitū   noster   circumventī sunt
2 A certain senator is trying to deceive you.
    senātōrī   quīdam   tē   dēcipit   cōnātur
    senātor   quidem   tuī   dēcipere cōnantur
3 He was lying hidden, in order to hear the old men's conversation.
    latēbat   ut   sermōnem senem   audīvisset
    latuerat   nē   sermō   senum   audīret
4 The same clients will be here tomorrow.
    eōsdem   cliēns   crās   aderunt
    eīdem   clientēs cotīdiē aberunt
5 The originator of the crime did not want to be seen in the forum.
    auctor   scelerī   in forum   vidēre   volēbat
    auctōrem sceleris in forō   vidērī   nōlēbat

The emperor's council

Among the people who took part in the government of the empire were the members of the emperor's 'cōnsilium' (council), often referred to as 'amīcī' (friends) of the emperor.

The consilium did not have a fixed membership; it was simply made up of those people whom the emperor invited to advise him on any particular occasion. Some men were regularly asked to meetings of the consilium; others were asked occasionally. Many would be experienced and distinguished men of senatorial rank, who had reached the top of the career described on pp.53–5. Some men of equestrian rank might also be invited, such as the commander of the praetorian guard. When there was a change of emperor, the new emperor usually invited some new members to meetings of the consilium, but also found it convenient to continue using some of the previous emperor's advisers. Often the new emperor had himself been a member of the previous emperor's consilium.

The matters on which the emperor asked his consilium for advice were naturally varied. The consilium might, for example, be summoned in moments of crisis, such as the discovery of a conspiracy against the emperor's life; or it might be consulted on the delicate question: 'Who should be the emperor's heir?' Sometimes the emperor would want advice about military decisions or foreign affairs. The story on pp.45–7, in which Domitian asks his advisers about Agricola's letter from Britain, is fictitious, but it would not have been odd or unusual for the consilium to have discussed such a question.

However, the commonest task of the amici was to advise the emperor while he was administering the law. For example, they might join him when he was hearing an appeal by a condemned prisoner, or settling a property dispute between two or more parties. After the people concerned had stated their case, the emperor would ask for the 'sententia' (opinion) of each member of the consilium in

Relief showing an emperor dealing with affairs of state, seated on a platform in front of the Basilica Julia in the forum

turn; he would then perhaps retire for further thought, and finally announce his decision. He was not bound to follow the majority opinion of the consilium, and could even ignore their advice altogether. In theory, the amici were free to give their opinions firmly and frankly; but under some emperors, it could be dangerous to speak one's mind too openly. During Domitian's reign a number of amici used their position as members of the consilium to increase their own power and to spread rumours and accusations about their enemies; it was said of one man that he could 'slit a throat with a whisper'.

Some of the cases which were heard by the Emperor Trajan are described by Pliny, who was sometimes invited to Trajan's consilium. They include a charge of adultery against a military tribune's wife and a centurion, and a dispute in a small town in Gaul where the local mayor had abolished the town's annual games. It is clear from Pliny's account that even quite trivial cases were sometimes referred to the emperor for decision; most Roman emperors were kept very busy, and needed the help of their amici in order to cope with the work-load.

The senatorial career

Most of the amici taking part in the discussion on pages 45–7 would have successfully followed a career known as the senatorial 'cursus honōrum' ('series of honours' or 'ladder of promotion') in which members of the senatorial class competed with each other for official posts in the Roman government. These official posts were arranged in a fixed order, and as a man worked his way through them, his responsibilities and status steadily increased. Some posts were compulsory, so that a man who had not held a particular post was not allowed to proceed to a higher one, except by special favour of the emperor. The most successful men got to the top, and the rest dropped out at various points along the way.

Some officials, such as the consuls, were chosen by the emperor; others were elected by the senate. Even in those posts where the choice was made by the senate, the emperor still had great influence, since he could 'recommend' particular candidates to the senate for election.

By the time of Domitian, the most important stages in the cursus honōrum were as follows:

1 *vīgintīvir* Every year twenty young men were chosen as 'vīgintīvirī', and served for a year in Rome as junior officials, assisting with such tasks as the management of the law courts and prisons, and the minting of the Roman coinage.
2 *tribūnus mīlitum* In the following year, each of the young men went abroad on military service as an officer in a legion.
3 *quaestor* On returning to Rome, a man who wanted to progress further in the cursus honorum would aim at the quaestorship. This post involved the management of sums of public money and was usually (but not always) held in Rome. It lasted for one year and was important because it qualified a man for entry into the senate, which met regularly to discuss and decide government business.
4 *tribūnus plēbis* or *aedīlis* After a compulsory interval of a year, an ex-quaestor who wanted further promotion had a choice. He might aim

to become one of the ten tribunes of the people, whose original responsibility had been to act as helpers and advisers of the common people (plēbs), but whose tasks had been greatly reduced by the time of Domitian. Alternatively, he could try to be appointed as one of the six aediles, who were responsible for the upkeep of public buildings, baths, sewers and roads.

5 *praetor* The chief task of the praetors was to run the Roman law courts. A man who had held the praetorship also became eligible for certain important posts abroad; for example, he might command a legion, or govern one of the twenty-eight provinces (except for the ten most important ones). Governorships of provinces were normally held for a period of three years.

6 *cōnsul* The highest post in the cursus honorum was the consulship. There were only two consuls at any one time, but they changed at intervals during the year. They presided at meetings of the senate, and had a general responsibility for supervising government business. The ablest ex-consuls became governors of the ten most important provinces; some men, through exceptional ability or by favour of the emperor, achieved further distinctions, including second or even third consulships.

Relief showing a magistrate in a mule-drawn chariot, followed by men carrying his sedan-chair

This system enabled the emperor to see who the ablest men were. It also showed him whether a man had any special skills which made him suitable for a particular job or province. For example, Agricola was a good soldier, while Pliny was an expert in financial matters; each man was given work that offered him opportunities to use his particular gifts. The careers of both men are given below. They differ from each other in the early stages, because Agricola did not become a vigintivir and had an unusually long period as a military tribune. Pliny's career looks somewhat fuller than Agricola's; this is partly because Agricola's governorship of Britain was exceptionally lengthy, and partly because Agricola held no post at all between his recall from Britain and his death.

Career of Agricola

A.D.

40	birth
58–61	tribunus militum in Britain
64	quaestor in Asia
66	tribunus plebis
68	praetor
70–73	legatus legionis XX in Britain
74–76	legatus (governor) of Aquitania
77	consul
78–84	legatus (governor) of Britain
93	death

Career of Pliny

A.D.

61 or 62	birth
?82	vigintivir (with responsibility for one of the law courts)
?83	tribunus militum in Syria
90	quaestor in Rome
92	tribunus plebis
93	praetor
94–96	praefectus aerarii militaris (in charge of the military treasury)
98–100	praefectus aerarii Saturni (in charge of the treasury of the god Saturn)
100	consul
103	augur (honorary priesthood, held simultaneously with other posts)
104–106	curator Tiberis (responsible for flood precautions, drainage, etc., in connection with river Tiber)
109–111	legatus Augusti in Bithynia (a special governorship by personal appointment of the emperor)
111	death

Several of the above dates, especially in the early part of Pliny's career, are approximate and uncertain.

Vocabulary checklist

amplius – more fully, at greater length
   amplissimus, amplissima, amplissimum – very great
aurum, aurī – gold
complūrēs, complūra – several
coniūnx, coniugis – wife
culpō, culpāre, culpāvī – blame
dignus, digna, dignum – worthy, appropriate
discō, discere, didicī – learn
dīvus, dīvī – god
dubitō, dubitāre, dubitāvī – hesitate, doubt
ēlātus, ēlāta, ēlātum – excited, carried away
exemplum, exemplī – example
exercitus, exercitūs – army
fīō, fierī, factus sum – become, be made
inānis, ināne – empty, meaningless
incēnsus, incēnsa, incēnsum – inflamed, angered
initium, initiī – beginning
invideō, invidēre, invīdī – envy, be jealous of
oblīvīscor, oblīvīscī, oblītus sum – forget
occāsiō, occāsiōnis – opportunity
odium, odiī – hatred
patria, patriae – country, homeland
paulō – a little
perturbō, perturbāre, perturbāvī, perturbātus – alarm, disturb
praefectus, praefectī – commander
proelium, proeliī – battle
revocō, revocāre, revocāvī, revocātus – recall, call back
satis cōnstat – it is generally agreed
sēcūrus, sēcūra, sēcūrum – without a care
validus, valida, validum – strong

nūptiae

When you have read this, answer the questions at the end.

Imperātōris sententia

in aulā Domitiānī, T. Flāvius Clēmēns, adfinis Imperātōris, cum Domitiānō
anxius colloquitur. Clēmēns semper cum Imperātōre cōnsentīre solet; verētur
enim nē idem sibi accidat ac frātrī Sabīnō, quī iussū Imperātōris occīsus est.

Domitiānus: decōrum est mihi, mī Clēmēns, līberōs tuōs hon-
5 ōrāre, nōn modo propter adfīnitātem nostram sed
etiam ob virtūtēs tuās. ego ipse, ut scīs, līberōs nūllōs
habeō quī imperium post mortem meam exerceant.
cōnstituī igitur fīliōs tuōs in familiam meam ascīscere.
cognōmina 'Domitiānum' et 'Vespasiānum' eīs dabō;
10 praetereā rhētorem nōtissimum eīs praeficiam, M.
Fabium Quīntiliānum. prō certō habeō Quīntiliānum
eōs optimē doctūrum esse.

'prō certō habeō Quīntiliānum eōs optimē doctūrum esse.' (lines 11–12)

Clēmēns:	grātiās maximās tibi agō, domine, quod fīliōs meōs
	tantō honōre afficis. ego semper –
Domitiānus:	satis! pauca nunc dē Pōllā, fīliā tuā, loquī velim. crēdō 15
	Pōllam quattuordecim annōs iam nātam esse. nōnne
	nōs oportet eam in mātrimōnium collocāre?
Clēmēns:	domine –
Domitiānus:	virum quendam cognōvī quī omnī modō fīliā tuā
	dignus est. commendō tibi Sparsum, senātōrem 20
	summae virtūtis quī magnās dīvitiās possidet.
Clēmēns:	at, domine, iam quīnquāgintā annōs nātus est
	Sparsus.
Domitiānus:	ita vērō! aetāte flōret.
Clēmēns:	at bis mātrimōniō iūnctus, utramque uxōrem 25
	repudiāvit.
Domitiānus:	prō certō habeō eum numquam cognātam Imper-
	ātōris repudiātūrum esse. quid multa? prōmittō
	Sparsum tibi generum grātissimum futūrum esse.
	haec est sententia mea, quam sī dissēnseris mūtābō. 30
	sed prius tibi explicandum erit quārē dissentiās.

adfīnis *relative, relation by marriage*
idem . . . ac *the same . . . as*
propter *because of*
adfīnitātem: adfīnitās *relationship*
virtūtēs: virtūs *virtue*
ascīscere *adopt*
cognōmina: cognōmen *surname,*
  additional name
afficis: afficere *treat*
quattuordecim *fourteen*

aetāte flōret: aetāte flōrēre *be in the prime of life*
bis *twice*
iūnctus: iungere *join*
utramque: uterque *each, both*
repudiāvit: repudiāre *divorce*
cognātam: cognāta *relative (by birth)*
quid multa? *in brief, in short*
generum: gener *son-in-law*
grātissimum: grātus *acceptable, pleasing*
mūtābō: mūtāre *change*

1 Why does Clemens normally take care to agree with Domitian?
2 What decision has Domitian taken about Clemens' sons? What
  arrangements does he intend to make about their education?
3 How old is Clemens' daughter Polla? What suggestion does
  Domitian make about her? Whom does he recommend, and on
  what grounds?
4 What two doubts does Clemens raise about Sparsus' suitability?
  How does Domitian answer Clemens' second objection?

Pōlla

Pōlla, fīlia Clēmentis, fortūnam suam queritur; māter Flāvia eam cōnsōlārī cōnātur.

Pōlla: quam crūdēlis est pater meus, quī mē Sparsō nūbere iussit! quid faciam, māter? num putās mē illī senī umquam
5 nūptūram esse? scīs mē alium quendam amāre.

Flāvia: ō dēliciae, nōlī lacrimāre! dūra est vīta; necesse est pārēre eīs quī nōs regunt. crēdō tamen Sparsum satis grātum et benignum tibi futūrum esse.

Pōlla: cūr mē ita dēcipis? scīs eum esse senem minimae
10 venustātis. scīs etiam eum duās uxōrēs iam repudiāvisse. at tū, māter, sententiā Imperātōris nimis movēris; nihil dē mē cūrās, nihil dē Helvidiō quem amō.

Flāvia: num tū tam audāx es ut istī amōrī indulgeās? iste enim Helvidius gentī nostrae est odiō. num oblīta es avum eius,
15 cum Vespasiānum Imperātōrem graviter offendisset, in exiliō occīsum esse? prūdēns estō, mea Pōlla! melius est cēdere quam frūstrā resistere.

queritur: querī *lament, complain about*	venustātis: venustās *charm*
cōnsōlārī *console*	movēris: movēre *move, influence*
nūbere *marry*	avum: avus *grandfather*
quid faciam? *what am I to do?*	estō! *be!*

Language note

1 Compare the following direct and indirect statements:

direct statements	indirect statements
'hostēs mox pugnābunt.'	crēdimus hostēs mox **pugnātūrōs esse**.
'The enemy will fight soon.'	We believe the enemy to be going to fight soon. or, in more natural English: We believe that the enemy will fight soon.

'senex perībit.'   medicus dīcit senem **peritūrum esse**.

'The old man will die.'   The doctor says that the old man will die.

The form of the verb in heavy print is known as the *future active infinitive*.

2 Further examples:

1 'multī āthlētae crās certābunt.'
2 praecō dīcit multōs āthlētās crās certātūrōs esse.
3 'novae cōpiae mox advenient.'
4 mīlitēs crēdunt novās cōpiās mox adventūrās esse.
5 suspicor ancillam tē dēceptūram esse.
6 mercātor spērat sē magnās dīvitiās comparātūrum esse.

3 Study the way in which the future active infinitive is formed:

portātūrus esse   to be about to carry
doctūrus esse   to be about to teach
tractūrus esse   to be about to drag
audītūrus esse   to be about to hear

Notice that the future active infinitive contains a participle ('portātūrus', etc.) which changes its ending in the usual way to agree with the noun it describes:

puer dīcit imperātōrem crās **reventūrum** esse.
The boy says that the emperor will return tomorrow.

puer dīcit fēminās crās **reventūrās** esse.
The boy says that the women will return tomorrow.

prīdiē nūptiārum

nox est. crās nūptiae Pōllae et Sparsī celebrābuntur. Pōlla per hortum patris errat. crēdit sē sōlam esse; ignōrat Helvidium advēnisse. quī, hortum clam ingressus, Pōllam querentem audit; inter arborēs immōtus stat.

Pōlla: quid faciam? Helvidius trēs diēs iam abest, neque scio
5   quō ille ierit. intereā tōtam domum nostram videō ad
nūptiās meās odiōsās parārī. ō Helvidī, ēripe mē ex hīs
malīs!

Helvidius: *(subitō prōgressus)* id libenter faciam. nēmō mē
prohibēbit.

10 Pōlla: *(gaudiō et pavōre commōta)* Helvidī! quō modō hūc vēnistī?
sī hīc captus eris, interficiēris. fuge, priusquam pater
meus tē cōnspiciat!

Helvidius: fugiam vērō, sed nōn sine tē. fuge mēcum, mea Pōlla! tē
ex hīs malīs ēripiam, sīcut tū modo precābāris.

15 Pōlla: quō modō fugere possumus? tū ipse scīs mē semper
custōdīrī. nūptiās crāstinās nūllō modō vītāre possum.
parentēs, Imperātor, lēgēs mē iubent cōguntque Sparsō
nūbere.

Helvidius: minimē, mea Pōlla! tibi polliceor mē prius moritūrum
20   esse quam ille senex tē uxōrem dūcat. nōbīs procul ex
hāc urbe fugiendum est, ubi parentēs tuī nōs invenīre
numquam poterunt.

Pōlla: distrahor et excrucior. hūc amor, illūc pietās mē trahit.

Helvidius: nōlī timēre, mea Pōlla! tē numquam dēseram, semper
25   servābō.

Flāvia: *(intrā domum)* Pōlla! Pōlla, ubi es?

Pōlla: ēheu! ā mātre vocor. brevissimē dīcendum est. Helvidī,
tē amō, tē semper amābō. fugere tamen tēcum nōn
possum. crās mē Sparsus uxōrem dūcet.

30 Helvidius: *(īrā et amōre incēnsus)* ēn haec fidēs! simulās tē mē amāre,
rē vērā Sparsum amās. scīlicet dīvitiīs Sparsī corrupta
es; amōrem meum floccī nōn facis.

Flāvia: (*intus*) Pōlla! ubi es, Pōlla?

Pōlla: (*dolōre paene cōnfecta*) audī, mī Helvidī! haec ultima verba
tibi dīcō; nōn enim puto mē umquam tē iterum vīsūram 35
esse. crās ego Sparsō nūbam. est mihi nūlla spēs fugae.
sed quamquam Sparsus mē uxōrem ductūrus est, mī

prīdiē *the day before*
errat: errāre *wander*
odiōsās: odiōsus *hateful*
ēripe: ēripere *rescue, snatch away*
crāstinās: crāstinus *tomorrow's*
prius . . . quam *before*
uxōrem dūcat: uxōrem dūcere *take as a wife, marry*
distrahor: distrahere *tear apart, tear in two*
hūc . . . illūc *this way . . . that way, one way . . . another way*
pietās *duty*
intrā *inside*
simulās: simulāre *pretend*

Lovers from an Arretine vase

Helvidī, iūrō mē tē sōlum amāre, iūrō mē . . . . .
(*lacrimās retinēre frūstrā cōnātur*) tē semper amātūram . . .

40   amātū. . . . (*vōx dēficit.*)

Helvidius: (*dextram Pōllae arripiēns*) Pōlla, dēsine mē tēque torquēre!
deōs testor Sparsum tē uxōrem numquam ductūrum
esse. cōnfīde mihi, mea Pōlla! (*Pōllam ardenter amplexus,
Helvidius abit.*)

45 Pōlla: (*Helvidium abeuntem spectāns, utrum spēret an timeat incerta*)
dea Fortūna, servā eum!

iūrō: iūrāre *swear*
dēficit: dēficere *fail, die away*
dextram: dextra *right hand*
arripiēns: arripere *seize*
testor: testārī *call to witness*
ardenter *passionately*

Language note

1 In Stage 36, you met the *present* subjunctive:

incertus sum ubi Mārtiālis hodiē **recitet**.
I am not sure where Martial is reciting today.

2 In Stages 37 and 38, you have met sentences like these:

cognōscere volō quārē Domitiānus nōs **arcessīverit**.
I want to find out why Domitian has sent for us.

Pōlla nescit quō Helvidius **ierit**.
Polla does not know where Helvidius has gone.

The form of the verb in heavy print is the *perfect* tense of the subjunctive.

3 Further examples:

1 centuriō scīre vult num senex equum cōnspexerit.
2 crās cognōscēmus quantam pecūniam parentēs nōbīs relīquerint.
3 uxor mē cotīdiē rogat quārē hanc vīllam ēmerim.
4 incertī sumus utrum nautae perierint an superfuerint.

4 Compare the perfect subjunctive with the perfect indicative:

perfect indicative	*perfect subjunctive*
portāvī	portāverim
portāvistī	portāverīs
portāvit	portāverit
portāvimus	portāverīmus
portāvistis	portāverītis
portāvērunt	portāverint

Perfect subjunctive forms of 'doceō', 'trahō' and 'audiō' are given on p.140 of the Language Information section.

5 For the perfect subjunctive of irregular verbs, see p.145.

cōnfarreātiō

I

diēs nūptiārum adest. Pōlla, veste nūptiālī ōrnāta, in cubiculō suō stat. māter
eam īnspicit.

Flāvia: nunc tē verte ad mē, Pōlla! flammeum firmē
capitī superpositum est? (*Pōllam lacrimāre videt.*) ō
5 mea fīlia, tibi haud lacrimandum est; diē
nūptiārum nōn decet lacrimāre.

servus Clēmentis: (*ingressus*) domina, iussus sum vōs ad sacrificium
arcessere. dominus meus dīcit victimam iam
ēlēctam esse, haruspicēs parātōs adstāre.
10 nūntius quoque iam adest, quī dīcit Imperātōrem, comitante Sparsō, mox adventūrum
esse.

Flāvia: bene! nūntiā dominō tuō nōs statim ad ātrium
prōcessūrās esse.

15 *Flāvia et Pōlla ad ātrium prōcēdunt, ubi multī amīcī, familiārēs, clientēs iam*
adsunt. subitō ingēns clāmor oritur:

spectātōrēs: euge! euge! advenit Imperātor! advenit Sparsus!

intrat Sparsus, multīs comitantibus servīs; deinde ingreditur ipse Domitiānus.

spectātōrēs: fēlīciter! fēlīciter!

20 *Pōlla, valdē commōta, ad Sparsum dūcitur; dextrās sollemniter iungunt. deinde*
Domitiānus, ut Pontifex Maximus, prōcēdit ut sacrificium Iovī faciat.

Sparsus: cōnsīde in hāc sellā, mea Pōlla. tē fessam esse
videō. mox pontifex fīnem sacrificiīs faciet. tum
uxor mea fīēs.

25 *in mediō ātriō, victima ā Domitiānō sacrificātur; precēs Iovī et Iūnōnī*
offeruntur. Pōlla tamen adeō perturbātur ut precēs audīre vix possit; in mente
eius haerent illa verba ultima Helvidiī: 'deōs testor Sparsum tē uxōrem
numquam ductūrum esse.'

Sparsus: (*Pōllam perturbārī animadvertit.*) nōlī timēre, mea
30 Pōlla! nunc cōnfarreātiōnem celebrābimus.

Sparsus Pōllam perturbārī animadvertit. (line 29)

Domitiānus: (*lībum farreum Sparsō et Pōllae offerēns*) hoc lībum
               sacrum cōnsūmite!
Sparsus et Pōlla, iuxtā sedentēs, lībum sacrum cōnsūmunt.
Domitiānus: tacēte vōs omnēs, quī adestis! (*omnēs tacent.*) vōbīs
               prōnūntiō hanc virginem nunc in manum huius 35
               virī convenīre.
spectātōrēs: fēlīciter! fēlīciter!
Domitiānus: nunc cēdite testibus! tabulae nūptiālēs
               signandae sunt.
tabulīs signātīs, omnēs ad triclīnium prōcēdunt, ubi cēna sūmptuōsa parāta est. 40

cōnfarreātiō *wedding ceremony*   lībum farreum *cake made from grain*
nūptiālī: nūptiālis *wedding*   iuxtā *side by side*
flammeum *veil*   in manum . . . convenīre *pass into*
superpositum est: superpōnere *place on*   *the hands of*
oritur: orīrī *rise up*   tabulae nūptiālēs *marriage contract,*
fēlīciter! *good luck!*   *marriage tablets*
Iūnōnī: Iūnō *Juno (goddess of marriage)*

II

sōle occidente, servī Pōllam domum Sparsī dēdūcere parant, ubi Sparsus, prior profectus, iam eam exspectat. chorus musicōrum carmen nūptiāle cantāre incipit.

chorus: ō Hymēn Hymenaee, iō!
5   ō Hymēn Hymenaee!

Flāvia: mea fīlia, sīc tē amplexa valedīcō. valē, mea Pōlla, valē!
servī, ut mōs est, puellam ā mātre abripiunt. duo puerī, quī facēs ardentēs ferunt, Pōllam forās dēdūcunt. magnā comitante turbā pompa per viās prōgreditur.

10 chorus: tollite, ō puerī, facēs!
           flammeum videō venīre.
           ō Hymēn Hymenaee, iō!
           ō Hymēn Hymenaee!

occidente: occidere *set*
prior *earlier*
chorus *chorus, choir*
musicōrum: musicus *musician*

Hymēn
Hymenaee: Hymenaeus } *Hymen (god of weddings)*
abripiunt: abripere *tear away from*
forās *out of the house*

III

tandem pompa domum Sparsī, flōribus ōrnātam, advenit. quī, domō ēgressus,
Pōllam ita appellat:

Sparsus: siste! quis es tū? quō nōmine hūc venīs?

Pōlla: ubi tū Gāius, ibi ego Gāia.

quibus verbīs sollemnibus dictīs, Pōlla postēs iānuae oleō unguit, ut 5
fascinātiōnem āvertat. Sparsus intereā, prō iānuā stāns, grātulātiōnēs iocōsque
spectātōrum accipit. subitō magnus clāmor audītur; ē mediā turbā ērumpit
iuvenis, pugiōne armātus, quī praeceps in Sparsum ruit.

iuvenis: nunc morere, Sparse! (*Sparsum ferōciter pugiōne petit; quī*
         tamen, ācriter sē dēfendēns, bracchium iuvenis prēnsāre cōnātur.) 10

Sparsus: subvenīte! subvenīte!

ingēns strepitus oritur; servī accurrunt; aliī spectātōrēs Sparsō servīsque
subveniunt, aliī immōtī et obstupefactī stant. Pōlla tamen, iuvene Helvidiō
agnitō, pallēscit.

Sparsus: (*cum Helvidiō lūctāns*) festīnāte! festīnāte! 15

servī Helvidium, tandem comprehēnsum, firmē retinent.

Sparsus: (*exclāmāns*) illum agnōscō! Helvidius est, homō
         īnfestissimus gentī Imperātōris. eum ad Imperātōrem
         dūcite! prō certō habeō Domitiānum eī poenam
         aptissimam excōgitātūrum esse. (*Pōlla horrēscit.*) nōlī 20
         timēre, mea Pōlla! ille iuvenis īnsānus numquam iterum
         nōs vexābit. nunc tibi tempus est domum tuam novam
         intrāre.

Sparsus Pōllam bracchiīs tollit ut eam trāns līmen portet. Helvidius ad
Domitiānum abdūcitur. 25

siste: sistere *stop, halt*
sollemnibus: sollemnis *solemn, traditional*
postēs: postis *post, door-post*
fascinātiōnem: fascinātiō *the evil eye*
āvertat: āvertere *avert, turn away*
morere! *die!*
lūctāns: lūctārī *struggle*
excōgitātūrum esse: excōgitāre *invent, think up*
horrēscit: horrēscere *shudder*
abdūcitur: abdūcere *lead away*

Language note

1   In Stage 34, you met the *present passive infinitive*, used in sentences like these:

laudārī volō.   sonitus **audīrī** nōn poterat.
I want to be praised.   The sound was unable to be
                                               heard.

2   In Stage 38, you have met the present passive infinitive in indirect statements. Study the following examples:

direct statements   *indirect statements*
'vexāris.'   scio tē **vexārī**.
'You are annoyed.'   I know you to be annoyed.
                                                      or, in more natural English:
                                                      I know that you are annoyed.

'multī mīlitēs exercentur.'   audīmus multōs mīlitēs
                                                      exercērī.
'Many soldiers are being   We hear that many soldiers are
trained.'   being trained.

3   Further examples:

1   prō certō habeō cēnam splendidam in vīllā iam parārī.
2   'cōnsul morbō gravī afflīgitur.'
3   senātōrēs dīcunt cōnsulem morbō gravī afflīgī.
4   'fīliī Clēmentis ā Quīntiliānō cotīdiē docentur.'
5   audiō fīliōs Clēmentis ā Quīntiliānō cotīdiē docērī.
6   amīcus meus affirmat tē numquam ab Imperātōre laudārī, saepe culpārī.

Exercises

1 Complete each sentence with the right word and then translate.

   1 cognōscere volō ubi fīlius vester . . . . . (habitet, habitent)
   2 tot gemmās ēmistī ut nūllam pecūniam iam . . . . . (habeās, habeātis)
   3 strēnuē labōrāmus ut opus ante lūcem . . . . . (perficiam, perficiāmus)
   4 tam fessus est amīcus meus ut longius prōgredī nōn . . . . . . (possit, possint)
   5 senex nescit quārē puerī in viā . . . . . (clāmēs, clāmet, clāment)
   6 iterum vōs rogō num hunc virum . . . . . (agnōscam, agnōscās, agnōscātis)

2 In each pair of sentences, translate sentence 'a'; then change it from a direct statement to an indirect statement by completing sentence 'b', and translate again.

For example: a puer labōrat.
               b dominus putat puerum labōr. . . .
Translated and completed, this becomes:
a puer labōrat.   The boy is working.
b dominus putat puerum labōrāre.
   The master thinks that the boy is working.

  1a multae vīllae ardent!
  1b senex dīcit multās vīllās ard. . . .
  2a centuriō appropinquat.
  2b mīlitēs putant centuriōnem appropinqu. . . .
  3a medicus tēcum cōnsentit.
  3b crēdō medicum tēcum cōnsent. . . .

(continued)

In sentences 4–6, nouns as well as verbs have to be completed. Refer if necessary to the table of nouns on pp.126–7 of the Language Information section.

4a rēx in illā aulā habitat.
4b scio rēg. . . in illā aulā habit. . . .
5a servī iam dormiunt.
5b fūr crēdit serv. . . iam dorm. . . .
6a puella dentēs nigrōs habet.
6b Mārtiālis dīcit puell. . . dentēs nigrōs hab. . . .

Marriage

The average age for a Roman girl to marry was about thirteen or fourteen; men usually married in their late teens or early twenties. If the husband had been married previously, like Sparsus in the story on pp.58–9, there might be a wide age-gap between him and his wife.

The husband was normally chosen for the girl by her father or guardian. The law laid down that if the girl did not agree to the marriage, it could not take place; but probably few daughters would have found it very easy to defy their father's wishes. The girl's father would also negotiate with the family of her future husband about the 'dōs' (dowry); this was a payment (in money or property or both) made by the bride's family to the husband.

At the ceremony of betrothal or engagement (spōnsālia), the husband-to-be made a promise of marriage, and the father of the bride promised on his daughter's behalf; gifts were exchanged, and a ring was placed on the third finger of the girl's left hand, as in many countries nowadays. (There was a widespread belief that a nerve ran directly from this finger to the heart.) Family and friends were present as witnesses, and the ceremony was followed by a party.

Gold betrothal ring

Under Roman law, there were two different sorts of marriage. In the first, which was known as marriage 'cum manū', the bride ceased to be a member of her father's family and passed completely into the 'manus' (control) of her husband; any property she possessed became her husband's, and although he could divorce her, she could not divorce him. A couple could enter into marriage 'cum manū' in various ways; one was by an ancient ceremony known as 'cōnfarreātiō', in which the bride and bridegroom together ate a sacred cake made of 'far' (grain). This ceremony was only used by a few aristocratic families and had almost died out by the end of the first century A.D.; however, on pages 66–9, Polla is married by confarreatio because she is related to the Emperor Domitian.

By the first century, marriage 'cum manū' had become far less common than the other type of marriage, which was known as marriage 'sine manū'. In this type of marriage, the bride did not pass into the 'manus' of her husband; legally, she was still regarded as a member of her father's family (even though she was now no longer living with them); she could possess property of her own and she could divorce her husband. It was very easy for a couple to enter into marriage 'sine manū'; all they needed to do was to live together after declaring their intention of being man and wife.

Whether a couple became married 'cum manū' or 'sine manū', they usually celebrated their wedding with some of the many customs and ceremonies that were traditional among the Romans. Some of these are mentioned in the story of Polla's wedding to Sparsus on pages 66–9: the flame-coloured bridal veil (flammeum); the symbolic joining of hands (iūnctiō dextrārum); the sacrifice; the signing of the marriage contract, witnessed by the wedding guests;

the wedding feast at the bride's house; the ancient custom of pretending to pull the bride away from her mother by force; the torch-lit procession to the bridegroom's house; the wedding song; the traditional words spoken by the bride to her husband, 'ubi tū Gāius, ego Gāia' ('Where you are Gaius, I am Gaia'); the anointing of the doorposts with oil; the calling out of noisy greetings and coarse jokes to the bridegroom; and the custom of carrying the bride across the threshold of her new home. Other traditions and ceremonies included the careful arrangement of the bride's hair, parted with the point of a spear and then divided into six plaits; the presentation of fire and water by the bridegroom to the bride; and the undressing of the bride by 'mātrōnae ūnivirae' (women who had had only one husband).

The chief purpose of Roman marriage, as stated in marriage contracts and in various laws, was the obvious one of producing and bringing up children. The Roman government often made efforts to encourage marriage and large families; in particular, the Emperor Augustus introduced a law which laid down penalties for those who remained unmarried (for example, by forbidding them to receive legacies) and offered special privileges to married couples who produced three or more children. Nevertheless, the birthrate in Rome dropped steadily from the second century B.C. onwards, especially among the senatorial class.

A Roman wife had fewer legal rights than her husband. In the eyes of the law, she was under the authority of either her husband or her father (or guardian), depending on whether she had been married 'cum manū' or 'sine manū'. She could not vote in elections, take an active part in public or political life, sit on a jury, or plead in court. But in some ways a first-century Roman wife had more freedom than women in other countries, and enjoyed a higher status than they did. She was not restricted to the home, but could visit friends, go to the theatre and the baths, and accompany her husband to dinner-parties (unlike the women of classical Athens, for example). Her traditional day-to-day task – the running of the household – was regarded by most Romans as important and valuable, and a woman could gain great prestige and respect for the way in which this task was carried out; in many aristocratic and

Relief showing a mother suckling her child while the father looks on

wealthy families, running the house was a highly complicated and demanding job, involving the management and supervision of a large number of domestic slaves.

Our knowledge of Roman married life is very incomplete. We know far less about the poor than about the wealthy upper classes, and have hardly any information on married life from the wife's point of view, because most of what is written in Latin was written by men. Nevertheless, the writings of Roman authors include many references to married life. The following letter, for example, was written by Pliny to his wife Calpurnia:

'The strength of my longing for you is hard to believe. Love is the reason above all others. Another reason is that we are not used to being separated. I spend most of the night awake, picturing you. During the day, at the times when I usually come to see you, my feet guide me to your room; then I turn sadly back, sick at heart.'

Calpurnia was Pliny's third wife. At the time of their marriage, she was about fifteen and he was in his early forties. In another letter, he writes about Calpurnia:

'From sheer affection for me, she keeps copies of my speeches, reads them over and over again and even learns them by heart. She is tortured with worry when I appear in court, and is overcome with relief when the case is over. Whenever I give a recitatio, she listens from behind a curtain waiting eagerly for comments of approval. As for my poems, she sets them to music and sings them, taught not by some musician but by love, the best of teachers.'

A letter by Cicero describes an incident from the stormy relationship between his brother Quintus and Quintus' wife Pomponia:

'We lunched at Arcanum. When we got there, Quintus said, perfectly politely, "Pomponia, you invite the women, and I'll get the slave-boys together." There was nothing to be cross about, as far as I could see, either in what he said or the way he said it. But, within everyone's hearing, Pomponia replied, "What, me? I'm only a stranger here!" – just because Quintus had made arrangements for the lunch without telling her, I suppose. "There you are," said Quintus. "That's what I have to put up with every day." I hid my feelings. We sat down to eat; she refused to join us. Quintus sent her some food from the table; she sent it back. The following day, Quintus told me that she had refused to sleep with him and had continued to behave as she had done at lunch-time.'

Roman married life is also referred to in numerous inscriptions, set up in memory of husbands and wives. For example:

'Here lies Amymone, wife of Marcus, most good and most beautiful, wool-spinner, dutiful, modest, careful, chaste, home-loving.'

'I have written these words so that those who read them may realise how much we loved each other.'

'To my dearest wife, with whom I lived two years, six months, three days, ten hours.'

Vocabulary checklist

aptus, apta, aptum – suitable
bracchium, bracchiī – arm
certus, certa, certum – certain, infallible
   prō certō habēre – know for certain
clam – secretly, in private
commendō, commendāre, commendāvī, commendātus –
    recommend
cōnfectus, cōnfecta, cōnfectum – worn out, exhausted, overcome
cōpiae, cōpiārum – forces
dextra, dextrae – right hand
ēripiō, ēripere, ēripuī, ēreptus – rescue, snatch away
familia, familiae – household
grātus, grāta, grātum – acceptable, pleasing
ignōrō, ignōrāre, ignōrāvī – not know of
intrā – inside
iungō, iungere, iūnxī, iūnctus – join
lēx, lēgis – law
līmen, līminis – threshold, doorway
mēns, mentis – mind
nūbō, nūbere, nūpsī – marry
orior, orīrī, ortus sum – rise, arise
polliceor, pollicērī, pollicitus sum – promise
pontifex, pontificis – priest
prohibeō, prohibēre, prohibuī, prohibitus – prevent
queror, querī, questus sum – lament, complain about
regō, regere, rēxī, rēctus – rule
trāns – across
unguō, unguere, ūnxī, ūnctus – anoint, smear
vereor, verērī, veritus sum – be afraid, fear
vērō – indeed
vestis, vestis – clothing

studia

hērēdēs prīncipis

I

in aulā Imperātōris, duo puerī in studiīs litterārum sunt occupātī. alter puer,
Titus nōmine, fābulam nārrāre cōnātur; alter, nōmine Pūblius, intentē audit.
adest quoque puerōrum rhētor, M. Fabius Quīntiliānus. Titus Pūbliusque,
filiī Clēmentis ac frātrēs Pōllae, nūper hērēdēs Imperātōris factī sunt.

5 Titus: (*fābulam nārrāns*) deinde Iuppiter, rēx deōrum,
sceleribus hominum valdē offēnsus, genus mortāle
dēlēre cōnstituit. prīmō eī placuit dē caelō fulmina
spargere, quae tōtam terram cremārent. haesitāvit
tamen Iuppiter. 'sī enim', sibi inquit, 'flammae ad
10   caelum ā terrā ascenderint, nōnne nōs deī ipsī
eōdem ignī cremābimur?' dīversam ergō poenam
impōnere māluit; nimbōs ingentēs dē caelō
dēmittere cōnstituit ut genus mortāle dīluviō
perderet.

15 *Titō nārrante, iānua subitō aperitur. ingreditur Epaphrodītus. puerī anxiī inter*
sē aspiciunt; Quīntiliānus, cui Epaphrodītus odiō est, nihilōminus eum cōmiter
salūtat.

Quīntiliānus: libenter tē vidēmus, Epaphro –
Epaphrodītus: (*interpellāns*) salvēte, puerī. salvē tū, M. Fabī. hūc
20   missus sum ut mandāta prīncipis nūntiem. prīnceps
vōbīs imperat ut ad sē quam celerrimē contendātis.
Quīntiliānus: verba tua, mī Epaphrodīte, nōn intellegō. cūr nōs
ad Imperātōrem arcessimur?

Epaphrodītus, nūllō respōnsō datō, puerōs Quīntiliānumque per aulam ad
25 *Imperātōris tablīnum dūcit. puerī, timōre commōtī, extrā tablīnum haesitant.*
Quīntiliānus: (*timōrem suum dissimulāns*) cūr perturbāminī, puerī?
Pūblius: bonā causā perturbāmur. Imperātor enim nōs sine
dubiō castīgābit vel pūniet.
Quīntiliānus: nimis timidus es, Pūblī. sī prūdenter vōs gesseritis,
30   neque castīgābiminī neque pūniēminī.

'bonā causā perturbāmur.' (line 27)

studiīs: studium *study*
litterārum: litterae *literature*
genus mortāle *the human race*
fulmina: fulmen *thunderbolt*
cremārent: cremāre *burn, destroy by fire*
dīversam: dīversus *different*
nimbōs: nimbus *rain-cloud*
dīluviō: dīluvium *flood*
perderet: perdere *destroy*
prūdenter *prudently, sensibly*
vōs gesseritis: sē gerere *behave, conduct oneself*

II

Quīntiliānus et puerī, tablīnum ingressī, Domitiānum ad mēnsam sedentem
muscāsque stilō cōnfīgere temptantem inveniunt. Domitiānus neque respicit
neque quicquam dīcit. puerī pallēscunt.

	Domitiānus:	(*tandem respiciēns*) nōlīte timēre, puerī. vōs nōn
5		pūnitūrus sum – nisi mihi displicueritis. (*muscam*
		aliam cōnfīgit; dēnique, stilō dēpositō, puerōs subitō
		interrogat:) quam diū discipulī M. Fabiī iam estis?
	Titus:	(*haesitāns*) d-duōs mēnsēs, domine.
	Domitiānus:	nōbīs ergō tempus est cognōscere quid didicerītis.
10		(*ad Pūblium repente conversus*) Pūblī, quid heri
		docēbāminī?
	Pūblius:	versūs quōsdam legēbāmus, domine, quōs Ovidius
		poēta dē illō dīluviō fābulōsō composuit.
	Domitiānus:	Ovidius? fācundus vērō erat ille poēta. meritō tamen
15		ex Ītaliā relēgātus est; nam nōn modo vītam
		impūram ēgit sed etiam prīncipem offendit.
		(*Epaphrodītus rīdet.*) itaque, versibus Ovidiānīs heri
		lēctīs, quid hodiē facitis?
	Pūblius:	hodiē cōnāmur eandem fābulam verbīs nostrīs atque
20		ōrātiōne solūtā nārrāre.

muscās: musca *fly*
cōnfīgere *stab, skewer*
respicit: respicere *look up*
displicueritis: displicēre *displease*
didicerītis: discere *learn*
repente *suddenly*
fābulōsō: fābulōsus *legendary, famous*
fācundus *fluent, eloquent*
meritō *deservedly, rightly*
Ovidiānīs: Ovidiānus *of Ovid*
ōrātiōne solūtā: ōrātiō solūta *prose speech (i.e. instead of verse)*

Quīntiliānus: ubi tū nōs arcessīvistī, domine, Titus dē īrā Iovis
 nārrātūrus erat.

Domitiānus: fābula scīlicet aptissima! eam audīre velim. Tite,
 nārrātiōnem tuam renovā!

Titus: (*fābulam cūnctanter renovāns*) Iu-Iuppiter igitur 25
 Aquilōnem in ca-cavernīs Aeoliīs inclūsit, et Notum
 līberāvit. quī madidīs ālīs ēvolāvit; ba-barba nimbīs
 gravābātur, undae dē capillīs fluēbant. simulatque
 Notus ēvolāvit, nimbī dēnsī ex aethera cum ingentī
 fragōre effūsī sunt. sed tanta erat Iovis īra ut 30
 imbribus caelī contentus nōn esset; auxilium ergō ā
 frātre Neptūnō petīvit. quī cum terram tridente
 percussisset, illa valdē tremuit viamque patefēcit ubi
 undae fluerent. statim flūmina ingentia per campōs
 apertōs ruēbant. 35

Domitiānus: satis nārrāvistī, Tite. nunc tū, Pūblī, nārrātiōnem
 excipe.

Pūblius: iamque inter mare et tellūrem nūllum discrīmen
 erat; mare ubīque erat, neque ūlla lītora habēbat.
 hominēs exitium effugere cōnābantur. aliī montēs 40
 ascendērunt; aliī, in nāvibus sedentēs, per agrōs illōs

nārrātiōnem: nārrātiō *narration*
cūnctanter *slowly, hesitantly*
cavernīs: caverna *cave, cavern*
Aeoliīs: Aeolius *Aeolian*
inclūsit: inclūdere *shut up*
Notum: Notus *South wind*
gravābātur: gravāre *load, weigh down*
imbribus: imber *rain*
Neptūnō: Neptūnus *Neptune (god of the sea)*
tridente: tridēns *trident*
campōs: campus *plain*
excipe: excipere *take over*
tellūrem: tellūs *land, earth*
discrīmen *boundary, dividing line*

rēmigāvērunt quōs nūper arābant; hic suprā segetēs
aut tēcta vīllārum mersārum nāvigāvit; ille in
summīs arboribus piscēs invēnit. lupī inter ovēs
natābant; leōnēs fulvī undīs vehēbantur. avēs,
postquam terram diū quaerēbant ubi cōnsistere
possent, tandem in mare fessīs ālīs dēcidērunt.
capellae gracilēs –

Pūbliō hoc nārrantī Domitiānus manū significat ut dēsistat. diū tacet, puerīs
50 *anxiīs exspectantibus; tandem loquitur.*

Domitiānus: fortūnātī estis, Pūblī ac Tite; nam, ut decet prīncipis
hērēdēs, ab optimō rhētore docēminī, quī optima
exempla vōbīs prōposuit. sī vōs, puerī, causās vestrās
tam fācundē dīxeritis quam Ovidius versūs
55 composuit, saepe victōrēs ē basilicā discēdētis; ab
omnibus laudābiminī.

'ab omnibus laudābiminī.' (lines 55–6)

Titus: (*timore iam dēpositō*) nōnne ūna rēs tē fallit, domine?
nōs sumus hērēdēs tuī; nōnne igitur nōs, cum causās
nostrās dīxerimus, nōn saepe sed semper victōrēs
discēdēmus et ab omnibus laudābimur?   60

Quīntiliānus ērubēscit. Domitiānus, audāciā Titī obstupefactus, nihil dīcit.
tandem, rīdēns vel rīsum simulāns, puerōs rhētoremque dīmittit; deinde, stilō
resūmptō, muscās iterum captāre incipit.

rēmigāvērunt: rēmigāre *row*
arābant: arāre *plough*
hic . . . ille *this man . . . that man, one man . . . another man*
suprā *over, on top of*
aut *or*
mersārum: mergere *submerge*
piscēs: piscis *fish*
ovēs: ovis *sheep*
fulvī: fulvus *tawny*
capellae: capella *she-goat*
gracilēs: gracilis *graceful*
causās . . . dīxeritis: causam dīcere *plead a case*
fācundē *fluently, eloquently*
fallit: fallere *escape notice of, slip by*
resūmptō: resūmere *pick up again*
captāre *try to catch*

Language note

1 Study the following examples:

'hērēdēs prīncipis' nunc **appellāmur**.
We are now called 'heirs of the emperor'.

cavēte, cīvēs! ab hostibus **dēcipiminī**.
Be careful, citizens! You are being fooled by the enemy.

The words in heavy print are passive forms of the 1st and 2nd
persons plural.

2 Compare the active and passive forms of the 1st person plural:

	active	*passive*
present	portāmus	portāmur
	we carry	we are carried
future	portābimus	portābimur
	we shall carry	we shall be carried
imperfect	portābāmus	portābāmur
	we were carrying	we were being carried

Further examples:

1 superāmur, superābimur, superābāmur; monēmur, mon-
ēbimur, monēbāmur.
2 iubēmur, invītāmur, pūnīmur; servābimur, prohibēbimur,
salūtābimur; dūcēbāmur, laudābāmur, terrēbāmur.

3 Compare the active and passive forms of the 2nd person plural:

	active	*passive*
present	portātis	portāminī
	you carry	you are carried
future	portābitis	portābiminī
	you will carry	you will be carried
imperfect	portābātis	portābāminī
	you were carrying	you were being carried

Further examples:

1 docēminī, docēbiminī, docēbāminī; laudāminī, laudābiminī, laudābāminī.
2 incitāminī, mittiminī, monēminī; rogābiminī, iubēbiminī; audiēbāminī, superābāminī.

4 Further examples of 1st and 2nd person plural forms:

1 ā clientibus nostrīs cotīdiē salūtāmur.
2 hodiē dērīdēminī; crās honōrābiminī.
3 ab omnibus comitibus dēserēbāmur.
4 terrēmur, terrēminī; culpābimur, culpābiminī; mittēbāmur, mittēbāminī.

5 Compare the passive forms in paragraphs 1 and 2 with the forms of the deponent verb 'cōnor':

present	cōnāmur	we try	cōnāminī	you try
future	cōnābimur	we shall try	cōnābiminī	you will try
imperfect	cōnābāmur	we were trying	cōnābāminī	you were trying

Further examples of 1st and 2nd person plural forms of deponent verbs:

1 ubi vōs proficīscēbāminī, nōs regrediēbāmur.
2 templum ipsum mox cōnspicābimur.
3 loquimur, loquiminī; pollicēbimur, pollicēbiminī; precābāmur, precābāminī.

The story of the flood, told by Publius and Titus on pages 80–4 above, is based on the following lines written by the poet Ovid. When you have read them, answer the questions at the end. At the start of the extract, the god Jupiter is about to punish the human race for its wickedness.

versūs Ovidiānī

iamque erat in <u>tōtās</u> sparsūrus fulmina <u>terrās</u>*:
sed timuit, nē forte <u>sacer</u> tot ab ignibus <u>aethēr</u>
conciperet flammās, <u>longusque</u> ardēsceret <u>axis</u>.
<u>poena</u> placet <u>dīversa</u>, genus mortāle sub undīs
perdere et ex <u>omnī</u> nimbōs dēmittere <u>caelō</u>.   5

    prōtinus <u>Aeoliīs</u> Aquilōnem claudit in <u>antrīs</u>.
ēmittitque Notum; <u>madidīs</u> Notus ēvolat <u>ālīs</u>;
barba gravis nimbīs, <u>cānīs</u> fluit unda <u>capillīs</u>.
fit fragor; hinc <u>dēnsī</u> funduntur ab aethere <u>nimbī</u>.

    nec <u>caelō</u> contenta <u>suō</u> est Iovis īra, sed illum   10
caeruleus frāter iuvat auxiliāribus undīs.
ipse tridente suō terram percussit, at illa
intremuit mōtūque viās patefēcit aquārum.
<u>exspatiāta</u> ruunt per apertōs <u>flūmina</u> campōs.

conciperet flammās: concipere flammās *burst into flames*
ardēsceret: ardēscere *catch fire, blaze up*
axis *(arched) vault of heaven*
antrīs: antrum *cave*
cānīs: cānus *white*
fit: fierī *be made, occur*
hinc *then, next*
caeruleus *from the deep blue sea*
iuvat: iuvāre *help, assist*
auxiliāribus: auxiliāris *additional*
intremuit: intremere *shake*
exspatiāta: exspatiārī *extend, spread out*

---

* Some noun-and-adjective phrases, in which an adjective is separated by one word or more from the noun which it describes, have been underlined.

iamque mare et tellūs nūllum discrīmen habēbant: 15
omnia pontus erant, dēerant quoque lītora pontō.
occupat hic collem, <u>cumbā</u> sedet alter <u>aduncā</u>
et dūcit rēmōs illīc, ubi nūper arābat;
ille suprā segetēs aut <u>mersae</u> culmina <u>vīllae</u>
nāvigat, hic <u>summā</u> piscem dēprendit in <u>ulmō</u>.   20

nat lupus inter ovēs, <u>fulvōs</u> vehit unda <u>leōnēs</u>,
quaesītīsque diū terrīs, ubi sistere possit,
in mare <u>lassātīs</u> volucris vaga dēcidit <u>ālīs</u>.
et, modo quā <u>gracilēs</u> grāmen carpsēre <u>capellae</u>,
nunc ibi <u>dēfōrmēs</u> pōnunt sua corpora <u>phōcae</u>.   25

pontus *sea*
dēerant: dēesse *be lacking, be missing*
collem: collis *hill*
cumbā: cumba *boat*
aduncā: aduncus *curved*
illīc *there, in that place*
culmina: culmen *roof*
ulmō: ulmus *elm-tree*
nat: nāre *swim*
lassātīs: lassāre *tire, weary*
volucris *bird*
vaga: vagus *wandering*
quā *where*
grāmen *grass*
carpsēre = carpsērunt: carpere *chew, nibble, crop*
dēfōrmēs: dēfōrmis *ugly, inelegant*
phōcae: phōca *seal*

1 How did Jupiter at first intend to punish the human race? Why did he change his mind?
2 What action does Jupiter take in line 6 and the beginning of line 7 (prōtinus . . . Notum)? Why?
3 What happened when Neptune struck the earth with his trident?
4 Which detail or incident in lines 17–23 do you find you can picture most vividly?
5 Which word in line 25 is used by Ovid to contrast with 'gracilēs' in line 24?
6 Which seems to you to be the better description of Ovid's account: 'serious' or 'light-hearted'? Why?

Language note

1   In Stage 36, you met verse sentences like this:

exigis ut *nostrōs* dōnem tibi, Tucca, *libellōs*.
You demand that I should give you my books, Tucca.

The adjective 'nostrōs' is separated from the noun which it describes ('libellōs').

2   In Stage 39, you have met sentences in which one noun-and-adjective phrase is followed by another:

caeruleus frāter iuvat **auxiliāribus undīs**.
His brother from the deep blue sea helps him with additional waves.

Further examples:

1   *arbore* sub *magnā* **parva** latēbat **avis**.
2   *vertice* dē *summō* **liquidōs** mōns ēvomit **ignēs**.

liquidōs: liquidus *liquid*
ēvomit: ēvomere *spit out, spew out*

Study the pattern formed by the pairs of noun-and-adjective phrases in each of the above sentences. Similar patterns are often formed in English verse by rhymes at the ends of lines. For example:

A man he was to all the country *dear*,
And passing rich with forty pounds a *year*;
Remote from towns he ran his godly **race**,
Nor e'er had changed, nor wished to change his **place**.

3 You have also met sentences in which one noun-and-adjective phrase is placed inside another one:

nunc ibi **dēfōrmēs** pōnunt *sua corpora* **phōcae**.
Now the ugly seals rest their bodies there.

Further examples:

1 in **mediōs** vēnit *iuvenis fortissimus* **hostēs**.
2 cōnstitit ante **oculōs** *pulchra puella* **meōs**.

Compare the arrangement of the noun-and-adjective phrases in the above sentences with the arrangement of the rhyming lines in such verse as the following:

> Ring out, wild bells, to the wild **sky**,
>   The flying cloud, the frosty *light*;
>   The year is dying in the *night*;
> Ring out, wild bells, and let him **die**.

4 In each of the following examples, pick out the Latin adjectives and say which nouns they are describing:

1 aure meā ventī murmura rauca sonant.
The hoarse murmurs of the wind sound in my ear.
2 iam nova prōgeniēs caelō dēmittitur altō. (*Virgil*)
Now a new generation is being sent down from high heaven.
3 nōn fuit ingeniō Fāma maligna meō. (*Ovid*)
Fame has not been unkind to my talent.
4 agna lupōs audit circum stabula alta frementēs. (*Ovid*)
The lamb hears the wolves howling around the tall sheepfolds.
5 atque opere in mediō laetus cantābat arātor.
And the happy ploughman was singing in the middle of his work.
6 vincuntur mollī pectora dūra prece. (*Tibullus*)
Hard hearts are won over by soft prayer.

5   Translate the following examples:

1 *A cry for help*
   at puer īnfēlīx mediīs clāmābat in undīs.
2 *An echo*
   reddēbant nōmen concava saxa meum.
3 *Travel plans*
   nunc mare per longum mea cōgitat īre puella. (*Propertius*)
4 *Evening*
   maiōrēsque cadunt altīs dē montibus umbrae. (*Virgil*)

concava: concavus *hollow*

Pick out the adjectives in each example, and say which nouns they are describing.

Exercises

1   Study the form and meaning of the following verbs and nouns and give the meaning of the untranslated words:

nōmināre	nominate, name	nōmen	name
volvere	turn, roll	volūmen	roll of papyrus, scroll
certāre	compete	certāmen	
crīmināre	accuse	crīmen	
fluere		flūmen	
unguere	anoint, smear	unguentum	ointment
arguere	prove, argue	argūmentum	proof, argument
impedīre		impedīmentum	hindrance, nuisance
vestīre	clothe, dress	vestīmenta	
ōrnāre		ōrnāmentum	
torquēre		tormentum	

Match each of the following Latin nouns with the correct English translation:

Latin: blandīmentum, incitāmentum, cōnāmen, mūnīmentum, sōlāmen

English: effort, flattery, encouragement, comfort, defence

2 In each sentence, replace the noun in heavy print with the correct form of the noun in brackets, and then translate. Refer if necessary to the table of nouns on pp.126–7 of the Language Information section; you may also need to consult pp.156–83 to find out the genitive singular of 3rd declension nouns, as a guide to forming the other cases.

1 subitō Pōlla **Flāviam** vīdit. (māter)
2 nūntius **senī** epistulam trādidit. (dominus)
3 senātōrēs ad aulam **Domitiānī** contendēbant. (imperātor)
4 iuvenis **Agricolae** tōtam rem nārrāvit. (dux)
5 ingēns multitūdō **Rōmānōrum** in amphitheātrō con-
veniēbat. (cīvis)
6 poēta **audītōribus** paucōs versūs recitāvit. (fēmina)

3 Complete each sentence with the right word and then translate.

1 fessus sum! cotīdiē ā centuriōne labōrāre . . . . . . (iubeor,
teneor)
2 tū semper bene recitās; semper ā rhētore . . . . . . (parāris,
laudāris)
3 nōlī dēspērāre, mī amīce! mox . . . . . . (spectāberis,
līberāberis)
4 maximē gaudeō; crās enim ab Imperātōre . . . . . .
(honōrābor, vituperābor)
5 cum in urbe habitārem, strepitū continuō . . . . . . (audiēbar,
mittēbar, vexābar)
6 medicus tē sānāvit, ubi morbō gravī . . . . . . (afficiēbāris,
dēcipiēbāris, dūcēbāris)

4 In each pair of sentences, translate sentence 'a'; then change it from a direct statement to an indirect statement by completing sentence 'b', and translate again.

For example: a hostēs advēnērunt.
             b nūntius dīcit hostēs advēn. . . .
Translated and completed, this becomes:
  a hostēs advēnērunt.   The enemy have arrived.
  b nūntius dīcit hostēs advēnisse.
     The messenger says that the enemy have arrived.

In sentences 1–3, a perfect *active* infinitive is required. For examples of the way in which this infinitive is formed, see p.44, paragraph 3.

1a Imperātor sententiam mūtāvit.
1b cīvēs crēdunt Imperātōrem sententiam mūtāv. . . .
2a nautae nāvem ingentem comparāvērunt.
2b mercātor dīcit nautās nāvem ingentem comparāv. . . .
3a fabrī mūrum optimē refēcērunt.
3b putō fabr. . . mūrum optimē refēc. . . .

In sentences 4–6, a perfect *passive* infinitive is required. For examples of the way in which it is formed, see p.48, paragraph 3. Note that the first part of this infinitive (e.g. 'parātus' in 'parātus esse') changes its ending to agree with the noun it describes.

For example: a epistulae missae sunt.
             b crēdō epistulās miss. . . . . . .
Translated and completed, this becomes:
  a epistulae missae sunt.   The letters have been sent.
  b crēdō epistulās missās esse.
     I believe that the letters have been sent.

4a victima ā pontifice ēlēcta est.
4b spectātōrēs putant victimam ā pontifice ēlēct. . . . .
5a multī amīcī ad cēnam vocātī sunt.
5b sciō multōs amīcōs ad cēnam vocāt. . . . . . .
6a captīvus occīsus est.
6b mīlitēs dīcunt captīv. . . occīs. . . . . . .

Authors, readers and listeners

After a Roman writer had recited his work to his patron or friends, or to a wider audience at a recitatio, as decribed in Stage 36, he had to decide whether or not to make it available to the general public. If he decided to go ahead, his next step was to have several copies made. If he or his patron owned some sufficiently educated slaves, they might be asked to make copies for the author to distribute among his friends; or the author might offer his work to the booksellers, whose slaves would make a number of copies for sale to the public.

Most Roman booksellers had their shops in the Argiletum, a street which ran between the forum and the Subura. Books were fairly cheap; a small book of poems might cost 5 sesterces if it were an ordinary copy, 20 sesterces if it were a de-luxe edition made of high-quality materials. After the work had been copied, all money from sales of the book belonged to the booksellers, not to the author. We do not know whether the booksellers ever paid anything to an author for letting them copy his work.

One result of these arrangements for copying and selling books was that there was no such thing in Rome as a professional writer; no author could hope to make a living from his work. Some of the people who wrote books were wealthy amateurs like Pliny, who made most of his money as a landowner and wrote as a hobby; others like Martial, depended on patrons for support.

Sometimes the emperor became an author's patron. For example, the poets Virgil and Horace were helped and encouraged first by the Emperor Augustus' friend Maecenas, and then by Augustus himself. Other authors, however, got into trouble with the emperor. Ovid, for instance, was sent into exile by Augustus because he had been involved in a mysterious scandal in the emperor's own family, and because he had written a poem entitled *Ars Amatoria* (*The Art of Love*), a witty and light-hearted guide for young men on the conduct of love affairs. The *Ars Amatoria* greatly displeased Augustus, who had introduced a number of laws for the encouragement of respectable marriage (see p.74), and Ovid was exiled to a distant part of the empire for the rest of his life. Under later emperors such as Domitian, it was safest for an author to publish nothing at all, or else to make flattering remarks about the emperor in his work, like Martial in the story on p.22 (lines 11–14).

Some works of Latin literature reached a wide public. For example, thousands of people saw the comic plays of Plautus when they were performed in the theatre. But most Roman authors wrote for a small, highly educated group of readers who were familiar not only with Latin literature, but also with the literature of the Greeks.

Schoolboys like Publius and Titus in the story on pp.80–5 were introduced by their teachers to the study of both Greek and Roman authors. Quintilian, who wrote a book called *The Education of an*

Relief showing a rhetor and his pupils

In this school, the pupils have high-backed chairs like the master, instead of the usual wooden benches. Notice the two partly-unrolled papyrus scrolls, the case of writing materials held by the right-hand boy and the low platform for the master. Suggest a reason for the rather apologetic attitude of the right-hand boy.

Orator, gives a long list of recommended authors, adding comments on each one. For example, he says that: 'Ovid is light-hearted even on serious subjects, and too fond of his own cleverness, but parts of his work are excellent.'

In this way, Latin literature played an important part in Roman education. Roman education, in turn, played an important part in the writing of Latin literature. Most Roman authors had received a thorough training from a rhetor, who taught them how to express themselves persuasively, how to choose words that would have maximum effect on an audience, and how to organise a speech in accordance with fixed rules. This training had a great influence on the way Latin literature was written.

The most important difference between Latin and modern literature is that modern literature (except drama) is usually written for silent reading, whereas Latin literature was normally written to be read aloud. Two reasons for this have been mentioned already: firstly, the easiest way for an author to tell the public about his work was to read it aloud to them; secondly, most authors had received a long training in public speaking when they were young, and this affected the way they wrote. There is also a third reason: when a Roman read a book, he normally read it aloud, even if he was reading it to himself. (Reading silently was unusual. Saint Augustine was amazed when he saw it done, and wrote a brief description of it: 'cum legebat, oculi ducebantur per paginas et cor intellectum rimabatur, vox autem et lingua quiescebant.' – 'When he was reading, his eyes glided over the pages, and his heart searched out the meaning, but his voice and tongue were at rest.')

The fact that Latin literature was written for speaking aloud, and not for silent reading, made a great difference to the way Roman authors wrote. They expressed themselves in ways that would sound effective when heard, not just look effective when read. For example, suppose a Roman author wished to say, in the course of a story:

'The unfortunate boy did not see the danger.'

He might express this quite straightforwardly:

'puer īnfēlīx perīculum nōn vīdit.'

But he might, especially in poetry, prefer a more dramatic way of expressing himself. For instance, he might address the character in the story as if he were physically present, and put a question to him:

'heu, puer īnfēlīx! nōnne perīculum vidēs?'
'Alas, unfortunate boy! Do you not see the danger?'

On the printed page, especially in English translation, this style of writing may sometimes appear rather over-heated and exaggerated to a modern reader, but when read aloud in Latin the effect can be very different. To read Latin literature silently is like looking at the score of a piece of music: the reader gets some idea of what the piece is like, but it needs to be performed aloud for full effect.

Drawing (based on a relief) of a reader choosing a book from a shelf

Vocabulary checklist

arbor, arboris – tree
aut – or
cadō, cadere, cecidī – fall
campus, campī – plain
capillī, capillōrum – hair
discrīmen, discrīminis – (1) dividing line, (2) crisis
ergō – therefore
fallō, fallere, fefellī, falsus – deceive, escape notice of, slip by
fragor, fragōris – crash
genus, generis – race
hinc – from here, then, next
iuvō, iuvāre, iūvī – help, assist
littera, litterae – letter (of alphabet)
    litterae, litterārum – letter, letters (correspondence)
mēnsis, mēnsis – month
ōrātiō, ōrātiōnis – speech
perdō, perdere, perdidī, perditus – destroy
respiciō, respicere, respexī – look back, look up
simulō, simulāre, simulāvī, simulātus – pretend
spargō, spargere, sparsī, sparsus – scatter
stilus, stilī – pen (pointed stick for writing on wax tablet)
studium, studiī – enthusiasm, study
suprā – over, on top of
ūllus, ūlla, ūllum – any

Numbers

ūnus – one	prīmus – first
duo – two	secundus – second
trēs – three	tertius – third
quattuor – four	quārtus – fourth
quīnque – five	quīntus – fifth
sex – six	scxtus – sixth
septem – seven	septimus – seventh
octō – eight	octāvus – eighth
novem – nine	nōnus – ninth
decem – ten	decimus – tenth

ūndecim – eleven
duodecim – twelve
trēdecim – thirteen
quattuordecim – fourteen
quīndecim – fifteen
sēdecim – sixteen
septendecim – seventeen
duodēvīgintī – eighteen
ūndēvīgintī – nineteen

vīgintī – twenty
trīgintā – thirty
quadrāgintā – forty
quīnquāgintā – fifty
sexāgintā – sixty
septuāgintā – seventy
octōgintā – eighty
nōnāgintā – ninety
centum – a hundred
ducentī – two hundred

iūdicium

ingēns senātōrum multitūdō in cūriā convēnerat, ubi Gāius Salvius
Līberālis accūsābātur.

'multa scelera ā Salviō in Britanniā
commissa sunt.'

prīmus accūsātor affirmāvit
multa scelera ā Salviō in
Britanniā commissa esse.

'Salvius testāmentum rēgis fīnxit.'

secundus accūsātor dīxit
Salvium testāmentum rēgis
fīnxisse.

'innocēns sum.'

Salvius respondit sē innocentem esse.

accūsātiō

I

septimō annō Domitiānī prīncipātūs, C. Salvius Līberālis, quī
priōre annō fuerat cōnsul, ab Acīliō Glabriōne falsī accūsātus est.
quā rē imprōvīsā perturbātus, amīcōs statim cōnsuluit utrum
accūsātiōnem sperneret an dēfēnsiōnem susciperet.

5 Salviō rogantī quid esset agendum, aliī alia suādēbant. aliī
affirmāvērunt nūllum perīculum īnstāre quod Salvius vir magnae
auctōritātis esset. aliī exīstimābant Domitiānī īram magis
timendam esse quam minās accūsantium; Salvium hortābantur ut
ad Imperātōrem īret veniamque peteret. amīcīs dīversa mon-
10 entibus, Salvius exspectāre cōnstituit, dum cognōsceret quid
Domitiānus sentīret.

interim Glabriō et aliī accūsātōrēs causam parābant. eīs magnō
auxiliō erat L. Mārcius Memor, haruspex et Salviī cliēns, quī,
socius quondam scelerum Salviī, nunc ad eum prōdendum
15 adductus est, spē praemiī vel metū poenārum. quō testimōniō ūsī,
accūsātōrēs rem ad Imperātōrem rettulērunt.

Domitiānus, ubi verba accūsātōrum audīvit, cautē sē gessit; bene
enim sciēbat sē ipsum sceleribus Salviī implicārī. interim, ut
sollicitūdinem dissimulāret et speciem amīcitiae praebēret,
20 Salvium dōnīs honōrāvit, ad cēnam invītāvit, cōmiter excēpit.

accūsātiō *accusation*
prīncipātūs: prīncipātus *principate,*
  reign
falsī: falsum *forgery*
imprōvīsā: imprōvīsus *unexpected,*
  unforeseen
sperneret: spernere *ignore*
dēfēnsiōnem: dēfēnsiō *defence*
aliī alia . . . *different people . . .*
  different things; some . . .
  one thing, some . . . another

īnstāre *be pressing, threaten*
minās: minae *threats*
interim *meanwhile*
accūsātōrēs: accūsātor *accuser,*
  prosecutor
socius *companion, partner*
ad eum prōdendum *to betray him*
testimōniō: testimōnium *evidence*
implicārī: implicāre *implicate, involve*
speciem: speciēs *appearance*

II

Domitia autem, iam ab exiliō revocāta atque in favōrem Domitiānī restitūta, intentē ultiōnem adversus Salvium meditābātur. patefēcerat enim Myropnous pūmiliō Salvium auctōrem fuisse exiliī Domitiae, Paridis mortis. Myropnous nārrāvit Salvium domum Hateriī falsīs litterīs Domitiam Paridemque invītāvisse; Salviō 5 auctōre, Domitiam in īnsulā duōs annōs relēgātam esse, Paridem occīsum esse.

accūsātōrēs igitur, ā Domitiā incitātī, cognitiōnem senātūs popōscērunt. invidia Salviī aucta est suspīciōne Cogidubnum venēnō necātum esse. fāma praetereā vagābātur reliquiās corporum 10 in thermīs Aquārum Sūlis repertās esse, dēfīxiōnēs quoque nōmine Cogidubnī īnscrīptās. quibus audītīs, multī crēdēbant Salvium animās inimīcōrum dīs īnferīs cōnsecrāvisse.

tum dēmum Salvius perīculōsissima esse haec crīmina intellēxit. veste ergō mūtātā, domōs circumiit amīcōrum, quī in tantō perīculī 15 sibi auxiliō essent. omnibus autem abnuentibus, domum rediit, spē omnī dēiectus.

restitūta: restituere *restore*
adversus *against*
domum Hateriī *to Haterius' house*
cognitiōnem senātūs: cognitiō senātūs *trial by the senate*
invidia *unpopularity*
fāma *rumour*
vagābātur: vagārī *spread, go round*
reliquiās: reliquiae *remains*
repertās esse: reperīre *find*
dēfīxiōnēs: dēfīxiō *curse*
animās: anima *soul*
dīs īnferīs: dī īnferī *gods of the Underworld*
veste . . . mūtātā: vestem mūtāre *change clothing, i.e. put on mourning clothes*
circumiit: circumīre *go round, go around*
abnuentibus: abnuere *refuse*

cognitiō

diē dictā, magna senātōrum multitūdō ad causam audiendam in
cūriā convēnit. Salvius, iam metū cōnfectus, ad cūriam lectīcā
vectus est; fīliō comitante, manibus extentīs, Domitiānō lentē ac
suppliciter appropinquāvit. quī Salvium vultū compositō excēpit;
5 crīminibus recitātīs, pauca dē Salviō ipsō addidit: eum Vespasiānī
patris amīcum fuisse, adiūtōremque Agricolae ā sē missum esse ad
Britanniam administrandam. dēnique L. Ursum Serviānum,
senātōrem clārissimum, ēlēgit quī cognitiōnī praeesset.

   prīmō diē cognitiōnis Glabriō crīmina levia et inānia exposuit.
10 dīxit Salvium domī statuam suam in locō altiōre quam statuam
prīncipis posuisse; imāginem dīvī Vespasiānī quae aulam rēgis
Cogidubnī ōrnāvisset ā Salviō vīlī pretiō vēnditam esse; et multa
similia. quibus audītīs, Salvius spērāre coepit sē ē manibus
accūsātōrum ēlāpsūrum esse.

15   postrīdiē tamen appāruit accūsātor novus, Quīntus Caecilius
Iūcundus. vōce ferōcī, vultū minantī, oculīs ardentibus, verbīs

īnfestissimīs Salvium vehementer oppugnāvit. affirmāvit Salvium superbē ac crūdēliter sē in Britanniā gessisse; cōnātum esse necāre Ti. Claudium Cogidubnum, rēgem populō Rōmānō fidēlissimum et amīcissimum; rēge mortuō, Salvium testāmentum fīnxisse; poenās maximās meruisse. 20

Quīntō haec crīmina expōnentī ācriter respondit Salvius: 'id quod dīcis absurdum est. quō modō venēnum Cogidubnō darī potuit, tot spectātōribus adstantibus? quis tam stultus cst ut crēdat mē mortem rēgis octōgintā annōrum efficere voluisse? etiam rēgēs mortālēs sunt.' dēnique servōs suōs ad tormenta obtulit; dē testāmentō nihil explicāvit. 25

subitō extrā cūriam īnfestae vōcēs sunt audītae clāmantium sē ipsōs Salvium interfectūrōs esse sī poenam scelerum effūgisset. aliī effigiem Salviī dēreptam multīs contumēliīs in Tiberim iēcērunt; aliī domum eius circumventam secūribus saxīsque pulsāre coepērunt. tantus erat strepitus ut ēmitteret prīnceps per urbem mīlitēs praetōriānōs quī tumultum sēdārent. 30

intereā Salvius, lectīcā vectus, ā tribūnō domum dēductus est; utrum tribūnus custōs esset an carnifex, nēmō sciēbat. 35

dictā: dictus *appointed*
ad causam audiendam *to hear the case, for the purpose of the case being heard*
suppliciter *like a suppliant, humbly*
adiūtōrem: adiūtor *assistant*
levia: levis *trivial*
exposuit: expōnere *set out, explain*
imāginem: imāgō *image, bust*
crūdēliter *cruelly*
amīcissimum: amīcus *friendly*
fīnxisse: fingere *forge*
meruisse: merērī *deserve*
dēreptam: dēripere *tear down*
sēdārent: sēdāre *quell, calm down*

Language note

1 From Stage 35 onwards, you have met sentences in which indirect statements are introduced by a verb in the present tense, such as 'dīcit', 'spērant', 'audiō', etc.:

direct statement	*indirect statement*
'custōs revenit.'	puer dīcit custōdem revenīre.
'The guard is returning.'	The boy says that the guard is returning.
'puella recitābit.'	spērant puellam recitātūram esse.
'The girl will recite.'	They hope that the girl will recite.
'vīllae dēlētae sunt.'	audiō vīllās dēlētās esse.
'The villas have been destroyed.'	I hear that the villas have been destroyed.

2 In Stage 40, you have met sentences in which indirect statements are introduced by a verb in the perfect or imperfect tense, such as 'dīxit', 'spērābant', 'audīvī', etc.:

direct statement	*indirect statement*
'custōs revenit.'	puer dīxit custōdem revenīre.
'The guard is returning.'	The boy said that the guard was returning.
'puella recitābit.'	spērābant puellam recitātūram esse.
'The girl will recite.'	They hoped that the girl would recite.
'vīllae dēlētae sunt.'	audīvī vīllās dēlētās esse.
'The villas have been destroyed.'	I heard that the villas had been destroyed.

Compare the indirect statements in paragraph 1 with the indirect statements in paragraph 2.

3 Further examples:

1 'Salvius multa scelera commīsit.'
2 accūsātōrēs affirmāvērunt Salvium multa scelera commīsisse.
3 'mīlitēs urbem facile capient.'
4 centuriō crēdēbat mīlitēs facile urbem captūrōs esse.
5 'Agricola iniūstē revocātus est.'
6 multī senātōrēs putābant Agricolam iniūstē revocātum esse.
7 'frāter tuus in Britanniā iam habitat.'
8 nūntius dīxit frātrem meum in Britanniā illō tempore habitāre.
9 'Domitiānus timōre coniūrātiōnis saepe perturbātur.'
10 cīvēs sciēbant Domitiānum timōre coniūrātiōnis saepe perturbārī.

When you have read section I, answer the questions that follow it.

dēspērātiō

I

intereā Rūfilla, Salviī uxor, dum spēs eius firma manēbat, pollicēbātur sē sociam cuiuscumque fortūnae futūram esse. cum autem sēcrētīs Domitiae precibus veniam ā prīncipe impetrāvisset, Salvium dēserere cōnstituit; dēnique mediā nocte ē marītī cubiculō
5 ēgressa domum patris suī rediit.

tum dēmum Salvius dēspērābat. fīlius Vitelliānus identidem affirmāvit senātōrēs numquam eum damnātūrōs esse; Salvium hortābātur ut animō firmō dēfēnsiōnem postrīdiē renovāret. Salvius autem respondit nūllam iam spem manēre: īnfestōs esse senātōrēs,
10 prīncipem nūllō modō lēnīrī posse.

illō tempore saepe in manibus Salviī vīsa est epistula quaedam. multī putābant mandāta sēcrēta Imperātōris in hāc epistulā continērī; fāma enim vagābātur Domitiānum ipsum Salviō imperāvisse ut Cogidubnum interficeret. amīcī Salvium
15 incitāvērunt ut hanc epistulam apud senātōrēs recitāret; ille tamen, fīliī salūtis memor, hoc cōnsilium reiēcit.

postulāvit tabulās testāmentī. quās signātās lībertō trādidit. tum frēgit ānulum suum, nē posteā ad aliōs accūsandōs ūsuī esset. postrēmō litterās in hunc modum compositās ad prīncipem mīsit:
20 'opprimor, domine, inimīcōrum coniūrātiōne mendācibusque testibus, nec mihi licet innocentiam meam probāre. deōs immortālēs testor mē semper in fidē adversus tē mānsisse. hoc ūnum ōrō ut fīliō meō innocentī parcās. nec quicquam aliud precor.'

dē Rūfillā nihil scrīpsit.

dēspērātiō *despair*	impetrāvisset: impetrāre *obtain*
dum *so long as*	reiēcit: reicere *reject*
firma: firmus *firm*	ūsuī esset: ūsuī esse *be of use*
sociam: socia *companion, partner*	mihi licet *I am allowed*
cuiuscumque: quīcumque *any, any whatever*	innocentiam: innocentia *innocence*

1 In what way did Rufilla's behaviour change? What caused this change? What effect did it have on Salvius?
2 What did Salvius' friends urge him to do, in order to clear himself of blame for Cogidubnus' death? Explain why he rejected their advice.
3 What did Salvius do after sealing and handing over his will? Explain his reason for doing this.
4 What was Salvius' only request in his last letter to the Emperor?

II

cum advesperāsceret, Salvius aliīs servīs pecūniam, aliīs lībertātem dedit. deinde mortem sibi cōnscīscere parāvit. venēnō ūtī nōn potuit; nam corpus iam diū antidotīs mūniēbātur. cōnstituit ergō vēnās pugiōne incīdere. quō factō, in balneum inlātus mox exanimātus est.   5

   at prīnceps, simulac mortem ā Salviō cōgitārī per ministrōs cognōvit, tribūnum mīlitēsque domum eius ēmīsit. mandāvit eīs ut Salviī mortem prohibērent; ipse enim crūdēlis vidērī nōlēbat. mīlitēs igitur, ā tribūnō iussī, Salvium ē balneō extrāxērunt, dēligāvērunt bracchia vulnerāta, sanguinem suppressērunt.   10

antidotīs: antidotum *antidote, remedy*
mūniēbātur: mūnīre *protect, immunise*
vēnās: vēna *vein*
incīdere *cut open*
suppressērunt: supprimere *staunch, stop flow*

damnātiō

postrīdiē Ursus Serviānus, quī cognitiōnī praefuerat, sententiam prōnūntiāvit: nōmen Salviī Fāstīs ērādendum esse; bonōrum eius partem pūblicandam, partem fīliō trādendam; Salvium ipsum quīnque annōs relēgandum.

5 ille igitur, vulneribus sānātīs, Rōmā discessit. eōdem diē mīrum fideī exemplum oculīs populī Rōmānī obiectum est. Q. Haterius Latrōniānus, quī favōrem Salviī flōrentis semper quaerēbat, eum rēbus adversīs oppressum nōn dēseruit, sed in exilium comitātus est.

10 paucīs post diēbus Domitiānus accūsātōribus honōrēs ac praemia distribuit. Glabriōnī sacerdōtium dedit; plūrimī autem exīstimābant Glabriōnem rē vērā Domitiānum hāc accūsātiōne graviter offendisse. Quīntō Caeciliō prīnceps favōrem suum ad honōrēs petendōs pollicitus est; simul autem eum monuit nē nimis
15 ēlātus vel superbus fieret. pūmiliōnī Myropnoō, quī Salviī scelera Domitiae patefēcerat, lībertātem obtulit; quam tamen ille recūsāvit. 'quid mihi cum lībertāte?' rogāvit; 'satis est mihi amīcum mortuum vindicāvisse.' et tībiīs dēmum resūmptīs, exsultāns cantāre coepit.

damnātiō *condemnation*
sententiam: sententia *sentence*
prōnūntiāvit: prōnūntiāre *announce*
Fāstīs: Fāstī *the list of consuls*
bonōrum: bona *goods, property*
pūblicandam: pūblicāre *confiscate*
flōrentis: flōrēre *flourish*
distribuit: distribuere *distribute*
dēmum *at last*

Language note

1   In Stage 32, you met sentences like these:

mihi fābula nārranda est.   Haterius laudandus est.
I must tell a story.   Haterius should be praised.

In these examples, the gerundives 'nārranda' and 'laudandus' are being used with 'est' to indicate that (in the speaker's opinion) something *ought* to be done ('the story *ought* to be told', 'Haterius *ought* to be praised').

2   In Stage 40, you have met the gerundive used with 'ad', meaning 'for the purpose of . . .':

deinde Quīntus ad Salvium accūsandum surrēxit.
Then Quintus stood up for the purpose of Salvius being accused.
    or, in more natural English:
Then Quintus stood up to accuse Salvius.

mercātōrēs in portū ad nāvem reficiendam manēbant.
The merchants stayed in port for the purpose of their ship being repaired.
    or, in more natural English:
The merchants stayed in port to repair their ship.

3   Further examples:

1 Calēdoniī nūntiōs ad pācem petendam mīsērunt.
2 sculptor ingentem marmoris massam ad statuās faciendās comparāvit.
3 poēta ad versūs recitandōs scaenam ascendit.
4 Memor ad scelera Salviī patefacienda adductus est.
5 servōs in agrōs ad frūmentum colligendum ēmīsī.

Exercises

1 Match each adjective in the left-hand column with an adjective of the opposite meaning, taken from the right-hand column, and translate both words.

benignus	stultus
callidus	levis
dūrus	pessimus
falsus	malignus
fidēlis	dīligēns
gravis	mollis
lātus	nūllus
neglegēns	perfidus
optimus	angustus
ūllus	vērus

2 Translate each sentence into Latin by selecting correctly from the list of Latin words.

1 I was being looked after by a very experienced doctor.

ā medicō   perītiōre   cūrābam
prope medicum   perītissimō   cūrābar

2 The commander hopes that the messengers will return soon.

lēgātus   spērō   nūntiī   mox   revenīre
lēgātī   spērat   nūntiōs   nūper   reventūrōs esse

3 We hear that a new house is being built.

audīmus   domus   nova   aedificāre
audīvimus   domum   novam   aedificārī

4 The soothsayer advises you not to leave the city.

haruspex   tū   monet   ut   urbī   discēdās
haruspicem   tē   monēbat   nē   ex urbe   discēssissēs

5 After the conspiracy had been revealed (*two words only*), very many senators were condemned.

coniūrātiōnem patefactā   plūrimī   senātōrī   damnātī sunt
coniūrātiōne   patefactam   maximī   senātōrēs damnātus est

3 With the help of paragraph 8 on page 134 of the Language Information section, turn each of the following pairs into one sentence by replacing the word in heavy print with the correct form of the relative pronoun 'quī' and adjusting the word order so that the relative pronoun comes at the *beginning* of the relative clause; then translate. Check the gender of the noun if necessary by referring to pp.156–83.

For example: intrāvit medicus. senex **medicum** arcessīverat.
This becomes: intrāvit medicus, quem senex arcessīverat.
                       In came the doctor, whom the old man had sent for.

1 templum   nōtissimum   vīsitāvimus.   Domitiānus   ipse **templum** exstrūxerat.
2 prō domō cōnsulis stābat pauper. praecō **pauperī** sportulam trādēbat.
3 ille vir est Quīntus. pater **Quīntī** mēcum negōtium agere solēbat.
4 tribūnus catēnās solvit. captīvus **catēnīs** vīnctus erat.
5 praemium illīs puerīs dabitur. auxiliō **puerōrum**, fūr heri comprehēnsus est.

Roman law courts

At the beginning of the first century A.D., there were several different law courts in Rome, for handling different sorts of cases. If a Roman was charged with a criminal offence, he might find himself in one of a group of jury courts known as 'quaestiōnēs' (commissions of inquiry), each responsible for judging a particular crime, such as treason, murder, adultery, misconduct by governors of provinces, forgery and election bribery. If he was involved in a civil (i.e. non-criminal) case, such as a dispute over a legacy, or an attempt to gain compensation from his next-door-neighbour for damage to property, he would go first of all to a praetor. The praetor would inquire into the cause and nature of the dispute, then either appoint an individual judge (iūdex) to hear the case, or refer it to an appropriate court; inheritance cases, for example, usually went to the court of the centumviri.

By the time of Domitian, some further ways of handling law cases had been added. For example, a senator charged with a crime could be tried in the senate by his fellow-senators, like Salvius in the story on pages 106–14; and the emperor himself took an increasingly large part in administering the law (see pp.51–2). But the courts described in the previous paragraph continued to operate alongside these new arrangements.

In modern times, someone who has committed an offence is liable to be charged by the police and prosecuted by a lawyer who acts on behalf of the state; the system is supervised by a government department. In Rome, however, there were no charges by the police, no state lawyers and no government department responsible for prosecutions. If a man committed a crime, he could be prosecuted only by a private individual, not by a public official. Any citizen could bring a prosecution, and if the accused man was found guilty, there was sometimes a reward for the prosecutor.

The law courts played an important part in the lives of many Romans, especially senators and their sons. Success as a speaker in

MVNIFICENTIA.PII.SEXTI.P.M

Statue of a Roman making a speech

court was one of the aims of the long training which they had received from the rhetor. In the law courts, a Roman could make a name for himself with the general public, play his part as a patron by looking after any clients who had got involved with the law, and catch the eye of people (such as the emperor and his advisers) whose support might help him gain promotion in the cursus honorum.

119

Fame and prestige usually mattered more than financial reward to the men who conducted cases in the courts. For a long time, they were forbidden to receive payment at all from their clients. Later, they were permitted to accept a fee for their services, but this fee was regarded as an unofficial 'present', or donation, which the client was not obliged to pay and the lawyer was not supposed to ask for.

Roman courts were probably at their liveliest in the first century B.C., when rival politicians fought each other fiercely in the courts as part of their struggle for power. By the time of Domitian, some of the glamour had faded; now that Rome was ruled by an emperor, there was less political power to be fought for. Nevertheless, the contests in court still mattered to the speakers and their clients, and attracted enthusiastic audiences. Pliny gives a vivid description of a case that aroused particularly lively interest:

> 'There they were, one hundred and eighty jurors, a great crowd of lawyers for both plaintiff and defendant, dozens of supporters sitting on the benches, and an enormous circle of listeners, several rows deep, standing round the whole courtroom. The platform was packed solid with people, and in the upper galleries of the basilica men and women were leaning over in an effort to hear, which was difficult, and see, which was rather easier.'

The writings of Martial, Pliny and Quintilian are full of casual details which convey the liveliness and excitement of the courts: the gimmicky lawyer who always wears an eye-patch while pleading a case; the hired squad of spectators who applaud at the right moments in return for payment; the successful speaker who wins a standing ovation from the jury; the careful allocation of time for each side, measured by the water-clock; the lawyer with the booming voice, whose speech is greeted by applause not only in his own court but also from the court next door; the windbag who is supposed to be talking about the theft of three she-goats, but goes off into long irrelevant ramblings about Rome's wars with Carthage three hundred years ago; and the anxious wife who sends messengers to court every hour to find out how her husband is getting on.

It is difficult to say how fair Roman justice was. Some of the tactics used in Roman law courts had very little to do with the rights and wrongs of the case. An accused man might dress up in mourning or hold up his little children to the jury to arouse their pity. A speaker whose client was in the wrong might ignore the facts altogether, and try to win his case by appealing to the jury's emotions or prejudices, or by using irrelevant arguments. Sometimes a man might be accused and found guilty for political reasons; there were a number of 'treason trials' under Domitian, in which innocent men were condemned. However, the writings of such men as Pliny and Quintilian show that at least some Roman judges made an honest effort to be fair and just. Fairness in a Roman law court was partly the result of the laws themselves. Roman law developed over several centuries, and at its best it was careful, practical and immensely detailed; it became the basis of many present-day legal systems in Europe and North America.

This coin illustrates voting in the senate: in the centre, under a canopy, th presiding magistrate's chair; on the right the tablets used by the jurors (A and C); and on the left the urn into which they were cast

Vocabulary checklist

adversus – against
affirmō, affirmāre, affirmāvī – declare
amīcitia, amīcitiae – friendship
augeō, augēre, auxī, auctus – increase
auxiliō esse – be a help, be helpful
cōnsul, cōnsulis – consul (senior magistrate)
crīmen, crīminis – charge
cūria, cūriae – senate-house
dēmum – at last
   tum dēmum – then at last, only then
exilium, exiliī – exile
exīstimō, exīstimāre, exīstimāvī – think, consider
fāma, fāmae – rumour
fingō, fingere, fīnxī, fictus – pretend, invent, forge
flōreō, flōrēre, flōruī – flourish
interim – meanwhile
invidia, invidiae – jealousy, envy, unpopularity
levis, leve – light, slight, trivial
meditor, meditārī, meditātus sum – consider
minor, minārī, minātus sum – threaten
mūtō, mūtāre, mūtāvī, mūtātus – change
obiciō, obicere, obiēcī, obiectus – present, put in the way of, expose to
probō, probāre, probāvī – prove
prōdō, prōdere, prōdidī, prōditus – betray
similis, simile – similar
socius, sociī – companion, partner
suādeō, suādēre, suāsī – advise, suggest
tumultus, tumultūs – riot
ūtor, ūtī, ūsus sum – use
videor, vidērī, vīsus sum – seem

Language
Information

Contents

PART ONE: MORPHOLOGY (formation of words)

Nouns

1	*first declension*	*second declension*			*third declension*	
	f.	*m.*	*m.*	*n.*	*m.*	*m.*
SINGULAR						
nominative and vocative	puella	servus (*voc.* serve)	puer	templum	mercātor	leō
genitive	puellae	servī	puerī	templī	mercātōris	leōnis
dative	puellae	servō	puerō	templō	mercātōrī	leōnī
accusative	puellam	servum	puerum	templum	mercātōrem	leōnem
ablative	puellā	servō	puerō	templō	mercātōre	leōne
PLURAL						
nominative and vocative	puellae	servī	puerī	templa	mercātōrēs	leōnēs
genitive	puellārum	servōrum	puerōrum	templōrum	mercātōrum	leōnum
dative	puellīs	servīs	puerīs	templīs	mercātōribus	leōnibus
accusative	puellās	servōs	puerōs	templa	mercātōrēs	leōnēs
ablative	puellīs	servīs	puerīs	templīs	mercātōribus	leōnibus

	fourth declension		*fifth declension*	
	f.	*n.*	*m.*	*f.*
SINGULAR				
nominative and vocative	manus	genū	diēs	rēs
genitive	manūs	genūs	diēī	reī
dative	manuī	genū	diēī	reī
accusative	manum	genū	diem	rem
ablative	manū	genū	diē	rē
PLURAL				
nominative and vocative	manūs	genua	diēs	rēs
genitive	manuum	genuum	diērum	rērum
dative	manibus	genibus	diēbus	rēbus
accusative	manūs	genua	diēs	rēs
ablative	manibus	genibus	diēbus	rēbus

m.	m.	f.	n.	n.	n.	
						SINGULAR
cīvis	rēx	urbs	nōmen	tempus	mare	*nominative and vocative*
cīvis	rēgis	urbis	nōminis	temporis	maris	*genitive*
cīvī	rēgī	urbī	nōminī	temporī	marī	*dative*
cīvem	rēgem	urbem	nōmen	tempus	mare	*accusative*
cīve	rēge	urbe	nōmine	tempore	marī	*ablative*
						PLURAL
cīvēs	rēgēs	urbēs	nōmina	tempora	maria	*nominative and vocative*
cīvium	rēgum	urbium	nōminum	temporum	marium	*genitive*
cīvibus	rēgibus	urbibus	nōminibus	temporibus	maribus	*dative*
cīvēs	rēgēs	urbēs	nōmina	tempora	maria	*accusative*
cīvibus	rēgibus	urbibus	nōminibus	temporibus	maribus	*ablative*

2 Compare the genitive (and dative) singular 'diēī' with 'reī'. Have you noticed that the '-ē-' of 'diēī' has a long mark, but the '-e-' of 'reī' does not?

3 Compare the endings of 'mare' with those of 'nōmen' and 'tempus'. Have you noticed that in the ablative singular 'mare' has an '-ī' instead of '-e'? Other third declension neuter nouns whose nominative singular ends in '-e', such as 'conclāve' ('room') and 'cubīle' ('bed'), form their cases in the same way as 'mare'.

4 For the ways in which the different cases are used, see pp.147-8.

Adjectives

1 first and second declension:

	masculine	*feminine*	*neuter*
SINGULAR			
nominative and vocative	bonus (*voc.* bone)	bona	bonum
genitive	bonī	bonae	bonī
dative	bonō	bonae	bonō
accusative	bonum	bonam	bonum
ablative	bonō	bonā	bonō
PLURAL			
nominative and vocative	bonī	bonae	bona
genitive	bonōrum	bonārum	bonōrum
dative	⟶ bonīs ⟵		
accusative	bonōs	bonās	bona
ablative	⟶ bonīs ⟵		

	masculine	*feminine*	*neuter*
SINGULAR			
nominative and vocative	pulcher	pulchra	pulchrum
genitive	pulchrī	pulchrae	pulchrī
dative	pulchrō	pulchrae	pulchrō
accusative	pulchrum	pulchram	pulchrum
ablative	pulchrō	pulchrā	pulchrō
PLURAL			
nominative and vocative	pulchrī	pulchrae	pulchra
genitive	pulchrōrum	pulchrārum	pulchrōrum
dative	⟶ pulchrīs ⟵		
accusative	pulchrōs	pulchrās	pulchra
ablative	⟶ pulchrīs ⟵		

2 third declension:

	masc. and fem.	neuter	masc. and fem.	neuter
SINGULAR				
nominative and vocative	fortis	forte	fēlīx	fēlīx
genitive	⟶fortis⟵		⟶fēlīcis⟵	
dative	⟶fortī⟵		⟶fēlīcī⟵	
accusative	fortem	forte	fēlīcem	fēlīx
ablative	⟶fortī⟵		⟶fēlīcī⟵	
PLURAL				
nominative and vocative	fortēs	fortia	fēlīcēs	fēlīcia
genitive	⟶fortium⟵		⟶fēlīcium⟵	
dative	⟶fortibus⟵		⟶fēlīcibus⟵	
accusative	fortēs	fortia	fēlīcēs	fēlīcia
ablative	⟶fortibus⟵		⟶fēlīcibus⟵	

	masc. and fem.	neuter	masc. and fem.	neuter
SINGULAR				
nominative and vocative	ingēns	ingēns	longior	longius
genitive	⟶ingentis⟵		⟶longiōris⟵	
dative	⟶ingentī⟵		⟶longiōrī⟵	
accusative	ingentem	ingēns	longiōrem	longius
ablative	⟶ingentī⟵		⟶longiōre⟵	
PLURAL				
nominative and vocative	ingentēs	ingentia	longiōrēs	longiōra
genitive	⟶ingentium⟵		⟶longiōrum⟵	
dative	⟶ingentibus⟵		⟶longiōribus⟵	
accusative	ingentēs	ingentia	longiōrēs	longiōra
ablative	⟶ingentibus⟵		⟶longiōribus⟵	

Comparison of adjectives

		comparative	*superlative*
1	longus	longior	longissimus
	long	*longer*	*longest, very long*
	pulcher	pulchrior	pulcherrimus
	beautiful	*more beautiful*	*most beautiful, very beautiful*
	fortis	fortior	fortissimus
	brave	*braver*	*bravest, very brave*
	fēlīx	fēlīcior	fēlīcissimus
	lucky	*luckier*	*luckiest, very lucky*
	prūdēns	prūdentior	prūdentissimus
	shrewd	*shrewder*	*shrewdest, very shrewd*
	facilis	facilior	facillimus
	easy	*easier*	*easiest, very easy*

2   Irregular forms:

bonus	melior	optimus
good	*better*	*best, very good*
malus	peior	pessimus
bad	*worse*	*worst, very bad*
magnus	maior	maximus
big	*bigger*	*biggest, very big*
parvus	minor	minimus
small	*smaller*	*smallest, very small*
multus	plūs	plūrimus
much	*more*	*most, very much*
multī	plūrēs	plūrimī
many	*more*	*most, very many*

Note: 'plūs', the comparative form of 'multus' above, is a neuter noun, e.g. 'plūs pecūniae' 'more (of) money'.

3   The forms of the comparative adjective 'longior' are shown on p.129.

4   Superlative adjectives like 'longissimus' change their endings in the same way as 'bonus' (shown on p.128).

Comparison of adverbs

1   Study the way in which comparative and superlative *adverbs* are formed:

	comparative	*superlative*
lātē	lātius	lātissimē
widely	*more widely*	*most widely, very widely*
pulchrē	pulchrius	pulcherrimē
beautifully	*more beautifully*	*most beautifully, very beautifully*
fortiter	fortius	fortissimē
bravely	*more bravely*	*most bravely, very bravely*
fēlīciter	fēlīcius	fēlīcissimē
luckily	*more luckily*	*most luckily, very luckily*
prūdenter	prūdentius	prūdentissimē
shrewdly	*more shrewdly*	*most shrewdly, very shrewdly*
facile	facilius	facillimē
easily	*more easily*	*most easily, very easily*

2   Irregular forms:

bene	melius	optimē
well	*better*	*best, very well*
male	peius	pessimē
badly	*worse*	*worst, very badly*
magnopere	magis	maximē
greatly	*more*	*most, very greatly*
paulum	minus	minimē
little	*less*	*least, very little*
multum	plūs	plūrimum
much	*more*	*most, very much*

3   Translate the following examples:

1 mīlitēs nostrī fortius pugnāvērunt quam barbarī.
2 faber mūrum facillimē refēcit.
3 ubi strepitum audīvī, magis timēbam.
4 optimē respondistī, mī fīlī.

Pronouns

1 ego, tū, nōs and vōs ('I', 'you (sg.)', 'we', 'you (pl.)')

	singular		*plural*	
nominative	ego	tū	nōs	vōs
genitive	meī	tuī	nostrum	vestrum
dative	mihi	tibi	nōbīs	vōbīs
accusative	mē	tē	nōs	vōs
ablative	mē	tē	nōbīs	vōbīs

2 sē ('herself', 'himself', 'itself', 'themselves', etc.)

	singular	*plural*
nominative (no forms)		
genitive	suī ◄———————————	
dative	sibi ◄———————————	
accusative	sē ◄———————————	
ablative	sē ◄———————————	

3 hic ('this', 'these', etc.; also used with the meaning 'he', 'she', 'they', etc.)

	singular			*plural*		
	masculine	*feminine*	*neuter*	*masculine*	*feminine*	*neuter*
nominative	hic	haec	hoc	hī	hae	haec
genitive	——► huius ◄——			hōrum	hārum	hōrum
dative	——► huic ◄——			——► hīs ◄——		
accusative	hunc	hanc	hoc	hōs	hās	haec
ablative	hōc	hāc	hōc	——► hīs ◄——		

4 ille ('that', 'those', etc.; also used with the meaning 'he', 'she', 'they', etc.)

	singular			plural		
	masculine	feminine	neuter	masculine	feminine	neuter
nominative	ille	illa	illud	illī	illae	illa
genitive	⟶ illīus ◄			illōrum	illārum	illōrum
dative	⟶ illī ◄			⟶ illīs ◄		
accusative	illum	illam	illud	illōs	illās	illa
ablative	illō	illā	illō	⟶ illīs ◄		

5 ipse ('myself', 'yourself', 'himself', 'herself', etc.)

	singular			plural		
	masculine	feminine	neuter	masculine	feminine	neuter
nominative	ipse	ipsa	ipsum	ipsī	ipsae	ipsa
genitive	⟶ ipsīus ◄			ipsōrum	ipsārum	ipsōrum
dative	⟶ ipsī ◄			⟶ ipsīs ◄		
accusative	ipsum	ipsam	ipsum	ipsōs	ipsās	ipsa
ablative	ipsō	ipsā	ipsō	⟶ ipsīs ◄		

6 is ('he', 'she', 'it', etc; also used with the meaning 'that', 'those', etc)

	singular			plural		
	masculine	feminine	neuter	masculine	feminine	neuter
nominative	is	ea	id	eī	eae	ea
genitive	⟶ eius ◄			eōrum	eārum	eōrum
dative	⟶ eī ◄			⟶ eīs ◄		
accusative	eum	eam	id	eōs	eās	ea
ablative	eō	eā	eō	⟶ eīs ◄		

Notice again how forms of 'is' can be used with the relative pronoun 'quī':

id quod mihi nārrāvistī statim Imperātōrī nūntiābitur.
What you have told to me will be reported at once to the Emperor.

eīs quī tardī advēnērunt neque cibum neque pecūniam dabō.
To those who arrived late I shall give neither food nor money.

7   īdem ('the same')

	singular			plural		
	masculine	feminine	neuter	masculine	feminine	neuter
nominative	īdem	eadem	idem	eīdem	eaedem	eadem
genitive	⟶ eiusdem ⟵			eōrundem	eārundem	eōrundem
dative	⟶ eīdem ⟵			⟶ eīsdem ⟵		
accusative	eundem	eandem	idem	eōsdem	eāsdem	eadem
ablative	eōdem	eādem	eōdem	⟶ eīsdem ⟵		

8   quī ('who', 'which', etc.; also meaning, *at beginning of sentences,* 'this', 'that', 'he', etc.)

	singular			plural		
	masculine	feminine	neuter	masculine	feminine	neuter
nominative	quī	quae	quod	quī	quae	quae
genitive	⟶ cuius ⟵			quōrum	quārum	quōrum
dative	⟶ cui ⟵			⟶ quibus ⟵		
accusative	quem	quam	quod	quōs	quās	quae
ablative	quō	quā	quō	⟶ quibus ⟵		

Notice again the use of the *connecting relative* to begin a sentence:

rēx signum dedit. quod simulac vīdērunt, haruspicēs ad āram prōgressī sunt.
The king gave a signal. As soon as they saw it, the soothsayers advanced towards the altar.

cōnsul 'captīvīs parcere cōnstituī', inquit. quibus verbīs audītīs, senātōrēs plausērunt.
'I have decided to spare the prisoners', said the consul. On hearing these words, the senators applauded.

9 From Stage 17 onwards, you have met various forms of the word **quīdam**, meaning 'one', 'a certain':

	singular			plural		
	masculine	feminine	neuter	masculine	feminine	neuter
nominative	quīdam	quaedam	quoddam	quīdam	quaedam	quaedam
genitive	——→ cuiusdam ←——			quōrundam	quārundam	quōrundam
dative	——→ cuidam ←——			——→ quibusdam ←——		
accusative	quendam	quandam	quoddam	quōsdam	quāsdam	quaedam
ablative	quōdam	quādam	quōdam	——→ quibusdam ←——		

quōsdam hominēs nōvī, quī tē adiuvāre poterunt.
I know certain men, who will be able to help you.

subitō senātor quīdam, celeriter prōgressus, silentium poposcit.
Suddenly one senator stepped forward quickly and demanded silence.

Compare the forms of 'quīdam' with those of 'quī' in paragraph 8.

With the help of the table above, find the Latin for the words in italics in the following sentences:

1 *Certain* ladies were standing outside the senate-house.
2 We saw *one* soldier trying to escape.
3 I was staying at the house of *a certain* friend.

Verbs

Indicative active

1

first conjugation	second conjugation	third conjugation	third '-iō' conjugation	fourth conjugation
PRESENT (*'I carry', 'I am carrying', etc.*)				
portō	doceō	trahō	capiō	audiō
portās	docēs	trahis	capis	audīs
portat	docet	trahit	capit	audit
portāmus	docēmus	trahimus	capimus	audīmus
portātis	docētis	trahitis	capitis	audītis
portant	docent	trahunt	capiunt	audiunt
FUTURE (*'I shall/will carry', etc.*)				
portābō	docēbō	traham	capiam	audiam
portābis	docēbis	trahēs	capiēs	audiēs
portābit	docēbit	trahet	capiet	audiet
portābimus	docēbimus	trahēmus	capiēmus	audiēmus
portābitis	docēbitis	trahētis	capiētis	audiētis
portābunt	docēbunt	trahent	capient	audient
IMPERFECT (*'I was carrying', etc.*)				
portābam	docēbam	trahēbam	capiēbam	audiēbam
portābās	docēbās	trahēbās	capiēbās	audiēbās
portābat	docēbat	trahēbat	capiēbat	audiēbat
portābāmus	docēbāmus	trahēbāmus	capiēbāmus	audiēbāmus
portābātis	docēbātis	trahēbātis	capiēbātis	audiēbātis
portābant	docēbant	trahēbant	capiēbant	audiēbant

2 Translate each word, then change it from the singular to the plural, so that it means 'we shall ...' or 'they will ...' instead of 'I shall ...' or 'he will ...', and translate again:

1 portābit; traham; audiet; docēbō; capiam.
2 nāvigābō; mittet; faciam; persuādēbit; impediet.

3 For ways of checking whether a verb ending in '-ēs', '-et', etc. belongs to the *present* tense of a *second* conjugation verb or the *future* tense of a *third* or *fourth* conjugation verb, see paragraph 3 on p.155.

4

first conjugation	second conjugation	third conjugation	third '-iō' conjugation	fourth conjugation

PERFECT *('I have carried', 'I carried', etc.)*

portāvī	docuī	trāxī	cēpī	audīvī
portāvistī	docuistī	trāxistī	cēpistī	audīvistī
portāvit	docuit	trāxit	cēpit	audīvit
portāvimus	docuimus	trāximus	cēpimus	audīvimus
portāvistis	docuistis	trāxistis	cēpistis	audīvistis
portāvērunt	docuērunt	trāxērunt	cēpērunt	audīvērunt

FUTURE PERFECT *('I shall/will have carried', etc.; but often translated by an English present tense: 'I carry', etc.)*

portāverō	docuerō	trāxerō	cēperō	audīverō
portāveris	docueris	trāxeris	cēperis	audīveris
portāverit	docuerit	trāxerit	cēperit	audīverit
portāverimus	docuerimus	trāxerimus	cēperimus	audīverimus
portāveritis	docueritis	trāxeritis	cēperitis	audīveritis
portāverint	docuerint	trāxerint	cēperint	audīverint

PLUPERFECT *('I had carried', etc.)*

portāveram	docueram	trāxeram	cēperam	audīveram
portāverās	docuerās	traxeras	ceperas	audīverās
portāverat	docuerat	trāxerat	cēperat	audīverat
portāverāmus	docuerāmus	trāxerāmus	cēperāmus	audīverāmus
portāverātis	docuerātis	trāxerātis	cēperātis	audīverātis
portāverant	docuerant	trāxerant	cēperant	audīverant

Indicative passive

1 In Unit IIIB, you met the 3rd person forms of the present, future and imperfect passive tenses. The other forms of these tenses are introduced in Stage 35 (1st and 2nd persons singular) and Stage 39 (1st and 2nd persons plural). The complete tenses are as follows:

PRESENT *('I am carried', 'I am being carried', etc.)*

portor	doceor	trahor	capior	audior
portāris	docēris	traheris	caperis	audīris
portātur	docētur	trahitur	capitur	audītur
portāmur	docēmur	trahimur	capimur	audīmur
portāminī	docēminī	trahiminī	capiminī	audīminī
portantur	docentur	trahuntur	capiuntur	audiuntur

FUTURE *('I shall/will be carried', etc.)*

portābor	docēbor	trahar	capiar	audiar
portāberis	docēberis	trahēris	capiēris	audiēris
portābitur	docēbitur	trahētur	capiētur	audiētur
portābimur	docēbimur	trahēmur	capiēmur	audiēmur
portābiminī	docēbiminī	trahēminī	capiēminī	audiēminī
portābuntur	docēbuntur	trahentur	capientur	audientur

IMPERFECT *('I was being carried', etc.)*

portābar	docēbar	trahēbar	capiēbar	audiēbar
portābāris	docēbāris	trahēbāris	capiēbāris	audiēbāris
portābātur	docēbātur	trahēbātur	capiēbātur	audiēbātur
portābāmur	docēbāmur	trahēbāmur	capiēbāmur	audiēbāmur
portābāminī	docēbāminī	trahēbāminī	capiēbāminī	audiēbāminī
portābantur	docēbantur	trahēbantur	capiēbantur	audiēbantur

2 In paragraph 1 above, find the Latin for:

1 I am heard; I shall be taught; I was being dragged.
2 you (sg.) will be carried; you (sg.) were being heard; you (sg.) are taught.
3 we are taught; we were being carried.
4 you (pl.) are taken; you (pl.) will be dragged; you (pl.) are heard.

3

PERFECT *('I have been carried', 'I was carried', etc.)*

portātus sum	doctus sum	tractus sum	captus sum	audītus sum
portātus es	doctus es	tractus es	captus es	audītus es
portātus est	doctus est	tractus est	captus est	audītus est
portātī sumus	doctī sumus	tractī sumus	captī sumus	audītī sumus
portātī estis	doctī estis	tractī estis	captī estis	audītī estis
portātī sunt	doctī sunt	tractī sunt	captī sunt	audītī sunt

FUTURE PERFECT *('I shall/will have been carried', etc.; but often translated as an English present tense: 'I am carried', etc.)*

portātus erō	doctus erō	tractus erō	captus erō	audītus erō
portātus eris	doctus eris	tractus eris	captus eris	audītus eris
portātus erit	doctus erit	tractus erit	captus erit	audītus erit
portātī erimus	doctī erimus	tractī erimus	captī erimus	audītī erimus
portātī eritis	doctī eritis	tractī eritis	captī eritis	audītī eritis
portātī erunt	doctī erunt	tractī erunt	captī erunt	audītī erunt

PLUPERFECT *('I had been carried', etc.)*

portātus eram	doctus eram	tractus eram	captus eram	audītus eram
portātus erās	doctus erās	tractus erās	captus erās	audītus erās
portātus erat	doctus erat	tractus erat	captus erat	audītus erat
portātī erāmus	doctī erāmus	tractī erāmus	captī erāmus	audītī erāmus
portātī erātis	doctī erātis	tractī erātis	captī erātis	audītī erātis
portātī erant	doctī erant	tractī erant	captī erant	audītī erant

Note: The gender may be changed in the forms above, e.g. 'docta est' ('she has been taught') or 'portātum est' ('it has been carried').

Notice again that the future perfect passive, like the future perfect active, is often translated by an English present tense:

sī exercitus noster crās victus erit, hostēs oppidum capere poterunt.
If our army is defeated tomorrow, the enemy will be able to capture the town.

4 Translate each example, then change it from the pluperfect to the perfect tense, keeping the same person and number (i.e. 1st person singular, etc.), and translate again. For example, 'portātī erāmus' ('we had been carried') would become 'portātī sumus' ('we have been carried', 'we were carried').

doctus eram; portātī erant; captus erās; tractus erat; audītī erātis; damnātī erāmus; coāctus erās; factī erant.

Subjunctive active

1 In Stage 36, you met the PRESENT tense of the subjunctive:

first conjugation	second conjugation	third conjugation	third '-iō' conjugation	fourth conjugation
portem	doceam	traham	capiam	audiam
portēs	doceās	trahās	capiās	audiās
portet	doceat	trahat	capiat	audiat
portēmus	doceāmus	trahāmus	capiāmus	audiāmus
portētis	doceātis	trahātis	capiātis	audiātis
portent	doceant	trahant	capiant	audiant

2 IMPERFECT SUBJUNCTIVE

portārem	docērem	traherem	caperem	audīrem
portārēs	docērēs	traherēs	caperēs	audīrēs
portāret	docēret	traheret	caperet	audīret
portārēmus	docērēmus	traherēmus	caperēmus	audīrēmus
portārētis	docērētis	traherētis	caperētis	audīrētis
portārent	docērent	traherent	caperent	audīrent

3 In Stage 38, you met the PERFECT tense of the subjunctive:

portāverim	docuerim	trāxerim	cēperim	audīverim
portāverīs	docuerīs	trāxerīs	cēperīs	audīverīs
portāverit	docuerit	trāxerit	cēperit	audīverit
portāverīmus	docuerīmus	trāxerīmus	cēperīmus	audīverīmus
portāverītis	docuerītis	trāxerītis	cēperītis	audīverītis
portāverint	docuerint	trāxerint	cēperint	audīverint

4 PLUPERFECT SUBJUNCTIVE

portāvissem	docuissem	trāxissem	cēpissem	audīvissem
portāvissēs	docuissēs	trāxissēs	cēpissēs	audīvissēs
portāvisset	docuisset	trāxisset	cēpisset	audīvisset
portāvissēmus	docuissēmus	trāxissēmus	cēpissēmus	audīvissēmus
portāvissētis	docuissētis	trāxissētis	cēpissētis	audīvissētis
portāvissent	docuissent	trāxissent	cēpissent	audīvissent

5 For ways in which the subjunctive is used, see pp.150–2.

Other forms of the verb

1 IMPERATIVE SINGULAR AND PLURAL (*'carry!' 'teach!'* etc.)

portā, portāte   docē, docēte   trahe, trahite   cape, capite   audī, audīte

2 PRESENT PARTICIPLE (*'carrying', 'teaching', etc.*)

portāns   docēns   trahēns   capiēns   audiēns

Present participles change their endings in the same way as 'ingēns' (shown on p.129), except that their ablative singular sometimes ends in '-e', e.g. 'portante', 'docente'.

3 PERFECT PASSIVE PARTICIPLE (*'having been carried', 'having been taught', etc.*)

portātus   doctus   tractus   captus   audītus

For perfect *active* participles, see Deponent verbs, p.143.

4 FUTURE PARTICIPLE (*'about to carry', 'about to teach', etc.*)

portātūrus   doctūrus   tractūrus   captūrus   audītūrus

Perfect passive and future participles change their endings in the same way as 'bonus' (shown on p.128).

5 PRESENT ACTIVE INFINITIVE (*'to carry', 'to teach', etc.*)

portāre   docēre   trahere   capere   audīre

6 PRESENT PASSIVE INFINITIVE (*'to be carried', 'to be taught', etc.*)

portārī   docērī   trahī   capı   audīrī

7 PERFECT ACTIVE INFINITIVE (*'to have carried', 'to have taught', etc.*)

portāvisse   docuisse   trāxisse   cēpisse   audīvisse

8 PERFECT PASSIVE INFINITIVE (*'to have been carried', 'to have been taught', etc.*)

portātus esse   doctus esse   tractus esse   captus esse   audītus esse

9 FUTURE ACTIVE INFINITIVE (*'to be about to carry', 'to be about to teach', etc.*)

portātūrus esse   doctūrus esse   tractūrus esse   captūrus esse   audītūrus esse

For examples of ways in which infinitives are used to express indirect statements, see pp.152–3.

10 GERUNDIVE (see p.154 for ways in which the gerundive is used)

portandus   docendus   trahendus   capiendus   audiendus

Gerundives change their endings in the same way as 'bonus' (p.128).

Deponent verbs

1

PRESENT			
cōnor	*I try*	loquor	*I speak*
cōnāris	*you try*	loqueris	*you speak*
cōnātur	*s/he, it tries*	loquitur	*s/he, it speaks*
cōnāmur	*we try*	loquimur	*we speak*
cōnāminī	*you try*	loquiminī	*you speak*
cōnantur	*they try*	loquuntur	*they speak*

FUTURE			
cōnābor	*I shall/will try*	loquar	*I shall/will speak*
cōnāberis	*you will try*	loquēris	*you will speak*
cōnābitur	*s/he, it will try*	loquētur	*s/he, it will speak*
cōnābimur	*we shall/will try*	loquēmur	*we shall/ will speak*
cōnābiminī	*you will try*	loquēminī	*you will speak*
cōnābuntur	*they will try*	loquentur	*they will speak*

IMPERFECT			
cōnābar	*I was trying*	loquēbar	*I was speaking*
cōnābāris	*you were trying*	loquēbāris	*you were speaking*
cōnābātur	*s/he, it was trying*	loquēbātur	*s/he, it was speaking*
cōnābāmur	*we were trying*	loquēbāmur	*we were speaking*
cōnābāminī	*you were trying*	loquēbāminī	*you were speaking*
cōnābantur	*they were trying*	loquēbantur	*they were speaking*

PRESENT PARTICIPLE			
cōnāns	*trying*	loquēns	*speaking*

PRESENT INFINITIVE			
cōnārī	*to try*	loquī	*to speak*

2 Translate each word, then change it to the 3rd person singular, so that it means 'he . . .' instead of 'I . . . ' or 'you . . .', and translate again.

1 loquor; cōnāberis; loquēbāris.
2 hortābor; sequēbar; precābāris.

3

PERFECT

cōnātus sum	*I (have) tried*	locūtus sum	*I have spoken, I spoke*
cōnātus es	*you (have) tried*	locūtus es	*you have spoken, you spoke*
cōnātus est	*he (has) tried*	locūtus est	*he has spoken, he spoke*
cōnātī sumus	*we (have) tried*	locūtī sumus	*we have spoken, we spoke*
cōnātī estis	*you (have) tried*	locūtī estis	*you have spoken, you spoke*
cōnātī sunt	*they (have) tried*	locūtī sunt	*they have spoken, they spoke*

FUTURE PERFECT

cōnātus erō	*I shall/will have tried*	locūtus erō	*I shall/will have spoken*
cōnātus eris	*you will have tried*	locūtus eris	*you will have spoken*
cōnātus erit	*he will have tried*	locūtus erit	*he will have spoken*
cōnātī erimus	*we shall/will have tried*	locūtī erimus	*we shall/will have spoken*
cōnātī eritis	*you will have tried*	locūtī eritis	*you will have spoken*
cōnātī erunt	*they will have tried*	locūtī erunt	*they will have spoken*

Note: The deponent future perfect, like other future perfects, is often translated as an English present tense: 'I try', 'I speak', etc.

PLUPERFECT

cōnātus eram	*I had tried*	locūtus eram	*I had spoken*
cōnātus erās	*you had tried*	locūtus erās	*you had spoken*
cōnātus erat	*he had tried*	locūtus erat	*he had spoken*
cōnātī erāmus	*we had tried*	locūtī erāmus	*we had spoken*
cōnātī erātis	*you had tried*	locūtī erātis	*you had spoken*
cōnātī erant	*they had tried*	locūtī erant	*they had spoken*

Note: The gender may be changed in the forms above, e.g. 'cōnāta est' ('she (has) tried') or 'locūtae sunt' ('they (females) spoke' or 'have spoken').

PERFECT ACTIVE PARTICIPLE

cōnātus	*having tried*	locūtus	*having spoken*

Perfect active participles change their endings in the same way as 'bonus' (shown on p.128).

PERFECT INFINITIVE

cōnātus esse	*to have tried*	locūtus esse	*to have spoken*

4 Translate each example, then change it from the pluperfect to the perfect tense, keeping the same person and number (i.e. 1st person singular, etc.) and translate again. For example, 'cōnātus erās' ('you (sg.) had tried') would become 'cōnātus es' ('you have tried', 'you tried').

locūtī erant; cōnātus eram; cōnātī erāmus; locūta erat; secūtī erant; adeptae erant; cōnāta eram.

Irregular verbs

1 *Indicative*

PRESENT *('I am', 'you are', etc.)*

sum	possum	eō	volō	nōlō	mālō	ferō
es	potes	īs	vīs	nōn vīs	māvīs	fers
est	potest	it	vult	nōn vult	māvult	fert
sumus	possumus	īmus	volumus	nōlumus	mālumus	ferimus
estis	potestis	ītis	vultis	nōn vultis	mālumus	fertis
sunt	possunt	eunt	volunt	nōlunt	mālunt	ferunt

FUTURE *('I shall/will be', etc.)*

erō	poterō	ībō	volam	nōlam	mālam	feram
eris	poteris	ībis	volēs	nōlēs	mālēs	ferēs
erit	poterit	ībit	volet	nōlet	mālet	feret
erimus	poterimus	ībimus	volēmus	nōlēmus	mālēmus	ferēmus
eritis	poteritis	ībitis	volētis	nōlētis	mālētis	ferētis
erunt	poterunt	ībunt	volent	nōlent	mālent	ferent

IMPERFECT *('I was', 'I could', 'I was going', etc.)*

eram	poteram	ībam	volēbam	nōlēbam	mālēbam	ferēbam
erās	poterās	ībās	volēbās	nōlēbās	mālēbās	ferēbās
erat	poterat	ībat	volēbat	nōlēbat	mālēbat	ferēbat
erāmus	poterāmus	ībāmus	volēbāmus	nōlēbāmus	mālēbāmus	ferēbāmus
erātis	poterātis	ībātis	volēbātis	nōlēbātis	mālēbātis	ferēbātis
erant	poterant	ībant	volēbant	nōlēbant	mālēbant	ferēbant

PERFECT *('I have been', or 'I was', etc.)*

fuī	potuī	iī	voluī	nōluī	māluī	tulī
fuistī	potuistī	iistī	voluistī	nōluistī	māluistī	tulistī
fuit	potuit	iit	voluit	nōluit	māluit	tulit
fuimus	potuimus	iimus	voluimus	nōluimus	māluimus	tulimus
fuistis	potuistis	iistis	voluistis	nōluistis	māluistis	tulistis
fuērunt	potuērunt	iērunt	voluērunt	nōluērunt	māluērunt	tulērunt

FUTURE PERFECT *('I shall/will have been', also often translated as 'I am', etc.)*

fuerō	potuerō	ierō	voluerō	nōluerō	māluerō	tulerō
fueris	potueris	ieris	volueris	nōlueris	mālueris	tuleris
fuerit	potuerit	ierit	voluerit	nōluerit	māluerit	tulerit
fuerimus	potuerimus	ierimus	voluerimus	nōluerimus	māluerimus	tulerimus
fueritis	potueritis	ieritis	volueritis	nōlueritis	mālueritis	tuleritis
fuerint	potuerint	ierint	voluerint	nōluerint	māluerint	tulerint

PLUPERFECT *('I had been', etc.)*

fueram	potueram	ieram	volueram	nōlueram	mālueram	tuleram
fuerās	potuerās	ierās	voluerās	nōluerās	māluerās	tulerās
fuerat	potuerat	ierat	voluerat	nōluerat	māluerat	tulerat
fuerāmus	potuerāmus	ierāmus	voluerāmus	nōluerāmus	māluerāmus	tulerāmus
fuerātis	potuerātis	ierātis	voluerātis	nōluerātis	māluerātis	tulerātis
fuerant	potuerant	ierant	voluerant	nōluerant	māluerant	tulerant

2 Subjunctive

PRESENT SUBJUNCTIVE

sim	possim	eam	velim	nōlim	mālim	feram
sīs	possīs	eās	velīs	nōlīs	mālīs	ferās
sit	possit	eat	velit	nōlit	mālit	ferat
sīmus	possīmus	eāmus	velīmus	nōlīmus	mālīmus	ferāmus
sītis	possītis	eātis	velītis	nōlītis	mālītis	ferātis
sint	possint	eant	velint	nōlint	mālint	ferant

IMPERFECT SUBJUNCTIVE

essem	possem	īrem	vellem	nōllem	māllem	ferrem
essēs	possēs	īrēs	vellēs	nōllēs	māllēs	ferrēs
esset	posset	īret	vellet	nōllet	māllet	ferret
essēmus	possēmus	īrēmus	vellēmus	nōllēmus	māllēmus	ferrēmus
essētis	possētis	īrētis	vellētis	nōllētis	māllētis	ferrētis
essent	possent	īrent	vellent	nōllent	māllent	ferrent

PERFECT SUBJUNCTIVE

fuerim	potuerim	ierim	voluerim	nōluerim	māluerim	tulerim
fuerīs	potuerīs	ierīs	voluerīs	nōluerīs	māluerīs	tulerīs
fuerit	potuerit	ierit	voluerit	nōluerit	māluerit	tulerit
fuerīmus	potuerīmus	ierīmus	voluerīmus	nōluerīmus	māluerīmus	tulerīmus
fuerītis	potuerītis	ierītis	voluerītis	nōluerītis	māluerītis	tulerītis
fuerint	potuerint	ierint	voluerint	nōluerint	māluerint	tulerint

PLUPERFECT SUBJUNCTIVE

fuissem	potuissem	iissem	voluissem	nōluissem	māluissem	tulissem
fuissēs	potuissēs	iissēs	voluissēs	nōluissēs	māluissēs	tulissēs
fuisset	potuisset	iisset	voluisset	nōluisset	māluisset	tulisset
fuissēmus	potuissēmus	iissēmus	voluissēmus	nōluissēmus	māluissēmus	tulissēmus
fuissētis	potuissētis	iissētis	voluissētis	nōluissētis	māluissētis	tulissētis
fuissent	potuissent	iissent	voluissent	nōluissent	māluissent	tulissent

3 Infinitives

PRESENT INFINITIVE (*'to be'*, *'to be able'*, *'to go'*, etc.)

esse	posse	īre	velle	nōlle	mālle	ferre

PERFECT INFINITIVE (*'to have been'*, *'to have been able'*, *'to have gone'*, etc.)

fuisse	potuisse	iisse	voluisse	nōluisse	māluisse	tulisse

FUTURE INFINITIVE (*'to be about to be'*, *'to be about to go'*, etc.)

futūrus esse	–	itūrus esse	–	–	–	lātūrus esse

4   Study the *passive* forms of 'ferō' and *irregular* forms of 'fīō':

PRESENT

feror	*I am (being) brought*	fīō	*I become (= I am being made)*
ferris	*you are (being) brought*	fīs	*you become*
fertur	*s/he, it is (being) brought*	fit	*s/he, it becomes*
ferimur	*we are (being) brought*	–	
feriminī	*you are (being) brought*	–	
feruntur	*they are (being) brought*	fīunt	*they become*

FUTURE

ferar	*I shall/will be brought*	fīam	*I shall/will become (= I shall be made)*
ferēris	*you will be brought*	fīēs	*you will become*
ferētur	*s/he, it will be brought*	fīet	*s/he, it will become*
ferēmur	*we shall/will be brought*	fīēmus	*we shall/will become*
ferēminī	*you will be brought*	fīētis	*you will become*
ferentur	*they will be brought*	fīent	*they will become*

IMPERFECT

ferēbar	*I was being brought*	fīēbam	*I was becoming (= I was being made)*
ferēbāris	*you were being brought*	fīēbās	*you were becoming*
ferēbātur	*s/he, it was being brought*	fīēbat	*s/he, it was becoming*
ferēbāmur	*we were being brought*	fīēbāmus	*we were becoming*
ferēbāminī	*you were being brought*	fīēbātis	*you were becoming*
ferēbantur	*they were being brought*	fīēbant	*they were becoming*

PERFECT

lātus sum	*I have been/was brought*	factus sum	*I have become, I became (= I was made)*
lātus es	*you have been/were brought*	factus es	*you have become, you became*
lātus est	*he has been/was brought*	factus est	*he has become, he became*
lātī sumus	*we have been/were brought*	factī sumus	*we have become, we became*
lātī estis	*you have been/were brought*	factī estis	*you have become, you became*
lātī sunt	*they have been/were brought*	factī sunt	*they have become, they became*

FUTURE PERFECT

lātus erō	*I shall/will have been brought*	factus erō	*I shall/will have become*
lātus eris	*you will have been brought*	factus eris	*you will have become*
lātus erit	*he will have been brought*	factus erit	*he will have become*
lātī erimus	*we shall/will have been brought*	factī erimus	*we shall/will have become*
lātī eritis	*you will have been brought*	factī eritis	*you will have become*
lātī erunt	*they will have been brought*	factī erunt	*they will have become*

PLUPERFECT

lātus eram	*I had been brought*	factus eram	*I had become (= I had been made)*
lātus erās	*you had been brought*	factus erās	*you had become*
lātus erat	*he had been brought*	factus erat	*he had become*
lātī erāmus	*we had been brought*	factī erāmus	*we had become*
lātī erātis	*you had been brought*	factī erātis	*you had become*
lātī erant	*they had been brought*	factī erant	*they had become*

PERFECT PASSIVE PARTICIPLE

lātus	*having been brought*	factus	*having become, having been made*

PRESENT PASSIVE INFINITIVE

ferrī	*to be brought*	fierī	*to become, to be made*

PERFECT PASSIVE INFINITIVE

lātus esse	*to have been brought*	factus esse	*to have become, to have been made*

PART TWO: SYNTAX (formation of sentences)

Uses of the cases

1 *nominative*

    rēx advēnit.   The king arrived.

2 *vocative*

    salvē, **amīce**!   Hello, friend!

3 *genitive*

    3a dux **mīlitum**   the leader of the soldiers

    3b nimis **aquae**   too much water

    3c homō **prāvī ingeniī**   a man of evil character

                                         (Compare 6b)

4 *dative*

    4a **nautīs** signum dedit.   He gave a signal to the soldiers.

    4b **centuriōnī** crēdēbam.   I trusted the centurion.

    4c Notice how the dative of 'auxilium', 'cūra' and 'odium' is used in the following examples:

        rēx nōbīs **magnō auxiliō**   The king was a great help to us.

           erat.

        dignitās tua mihi **cūrae** est.   Your dignity is a matter of

                                     concern to me.

        Epaphrodītus omnibus   Epaphroditus is hateful to

           odiō est.   everyone.

                 Or, Everyone hates Epaphroditus.

5 *accusative*

    5a **puerōs** laudāvī.   I praised the boys.

    5b **tōtam noctem**   We were sailing all night.

           nāvigābāmus.   (Compare 6d)

    5c prope **aulam**; inter **avēs**   near the palace; among the birds

                                         (Compare 6e)

(continued on p.148)

6 *ablative*

6a **īrā** incēnsus	inflamed by anger
6b puella **capillīs longīs**	a girl with long hair (Compare 3c)
6c **humilī gente** nātus	born from a humble family
6d **sextō diē** discessērunt.	They left on the sixth day. (Compare 5b)
6e cum **clientibus**; prō **templō**	with the clients; in front of the temple (Compare 5c)

6f Notice the following use of the ablative:

senex erat languidior **fīliō**, ignāvior **uxōre**.

The old man was feebler than his son and lazier than his wife.

Compare this with another way of expressing the same idea:

senex erat languidior quam fīlius, ignāvior quam uxor.

6g You have also met the ablative used with adjectives such as 'dignus' ('worthy') and 'plēnus' ('full'), and verbs such as 'ūtor' ('I use') and 'fruor' ('I enjoy'):

magnō honōre dignus	worthy of great honour
vītā quiētā fruēbar.	I was enjoying a quiet life.

For examples of ablative absolute phrases, see paragraph 5 on p.150.

7 Further examples of some of the uses listed above:

1 satis pecūniae habētis?
2 theātrum spectātōribus plēnum erat.
3 septem hōrās dormiēbam.
4 es stultior asinō!
5 mīlitēs gladiīs et pugiōnibus ūtēbantur.
6 Myropnous vōbīs auxiliō erit.

Uses of the participle

1   From Unit IIIA onwards, you have seen how participles are used to describe nouns or pronouns:

clientēs, sportulam adeptī, discessērunt.
The clients, having obtained their handout, departed.

centuriō tē in umbrā latentem vīdit.
The centurion saw you hiding in the shadow.

In the first example, the perfect active participle 'adeptī' describes 'clientēs'; in the second example, the present participle 'latentem' describes 'tē'.

2   Sometimes the noun or pronoun described by a participle is omitted:

valdē perturbātus, ex urbe fūgit.
Having been thoroughly alarmed, he fled from the city.

moritūrī tē salūtāmus.
We, (who are) about to die, salute you.

In examples like these, the ending of the verb ('fūg**it**', 'salūt**āmus**', etc.) makes it clear that the participle refers to 'he', 'we', etc.

3   Sometimes the participle refers not to a particular person or thing but more vaguely to 'somebody' or 'some people':

tū faciem sub aquā, Sexte, natantis habēs.
You have the face, Sextus, of (someone) swimming under water.

ārea plēna strepitū labōrantium erat.
The courtyard was full of the noise of (people) working.

(continued on p.150)

4 Notice again how a noun and participle in the dative case may be placed at the beginning of the sentence:

Salviō dē fortūnā querentī nūllum respōnsum dedī.
To Salvius complaining about his luck I gave no reply.
    or, in more natural English:
When Salvius complained about his luck, I gave him no reply.

5 In Unit IIIB, you met *ablative absolute* phrases:

senex, ratiōnibus subductīs, fīliōs arcessīvit.
After drawing up his accounts, the old man sent for his sons.

Epaphrodītō loquente, nūntius accurrit.
While Epaphroditus was speaking, a messenger came dashing up.

6 Further examples:

  1 flammīs exstīnctīs, dominus ruīnam īnspexit.
  2 ubīque vōcēs poētam laudantium audiēbantur.
  3 ā iūdice damnātus, in exilium iit.
  4 līberī, plūrimōs cāsūs passī, auxilium nostrum petēbant.
  5 servō haesitantī lībertātem pecūniamque obtulī.
  6 sōle oriente, lūx fīēbat.

Uses of the subjunctive

1 *with 'cum'*
servī, cum lectīcam dēposuissent, circumspectāvērunt.
When the slaves had put down the carrying-chair, they looked around.

2 *indirect question*
haruspicēs cognōscere cōnābuntur num ōmina bona sint.
The soothsayers will try to find out whether the omens are good.

3 *purpose clause*

Domitiānus ipse adest ut fābulam spectet.
Domitian himself is here to watch the play.

mīlitēs ēmīsit quī turbam dēpellerent.
He sent out soldiers to drive the crowd away.

4 *indirect command*

Agricola Britannōs hortātus est ut mōrēs Rōmānōs discerent.
Agricola encouraged the Britons to learn Roman ways.

ducem ōrābimus nē captīvōs interficiat.
We shall beg the leader not to kill the prisoners.

5 *result clause*

tantās dīvitiās adeptus est ut vīllam splendidam iam possideat.
He has obtained such great riches that he now owns a splendid villa.

6 *with 'priusquam' ('before') and 'dum' ('until')*

nōbīs fugiendum est, priusquam custōdēs nōs cōnspiciant.
We must run away before the guards catch sight of us.

exspectābant dum centuriō signum daret.
They were waiting until the centurion should give the signal.
   or, in more natural English:
They were waiting for the centurion to give the signal.

7 The following examples include all the six uses of the subjunctive listed above, and all the four subjunctive tenses (present, imperfect, perfect and pluperfect, listed on p.140):

1 senex, cum verba medicī audīvisset, testāmentum fēcit.
2 mīlitibus persuādēbō ut marītō tuō parcant.
3 latrōnēs mercātōrem occīdērunt priusquam ad salūtem pervenīret.
4 tam benignus est rēx ut omnēs eum ament.
5 scīre volō quis fenestram frēgerit.
6 dominus ad iānuam festīnāvit ut hospitēs exciperet.

(continued on p.152)

8 From Stage 37 onwards, you have met the subjunctive used in sentences like these:

avārus timēbat **nē fūr aurum invenīret**.
The miser was afraid that a thief would find his gold.

vereor **nē inimīcī nostrī tibi noceant**.
I am afraid that our enemies may harm you.

The groups of words in bold face are known as *fear clauses*.

Further examples:

1 timeō nē Britannī urbem mox capiant.
2 dominus verēbātur nē servī effugerent.

Indirect statement

1 From Stage 35 onwards, you have met *indirect statements*, expressed by a noun or pronoun in the *accusative* case and a verb in one of the following *infinitive* forms:

1 *present active infinitive*
   puto poētam optimē recitāre.
   I think that the poet recites very well.
   (Compare this with the direct statement:
   'poēta optimē recitat.')

2 *present passive infinitive*
   servus crēdit multōs hospitēs invītārī.
   The slave believes that many guests are being invited.
   (Compare: 'multī hospitēs invītantur.')

3 *perfect active infinitive*
   cūr suspicāris Salvium testāmentum fīnxisse?
   Why do you suspect that Salvius forged the will?
   (Compare: 'Salvius testāmentum fīnxit.')

4 *perfect passive infinitive*
   fāma vagātur multa oppida dēlēta esse.
   A rumor is going round that many towns have been destroyed.
   (Compare: 'multa oppida dēlēta sunt.')

5 *future active infinitive*
   crēdō mīlitēs fidem servātūrōs esse.
   I believe that the soldiers will keep their word.
   (Compare: 'mīlitēs fidem servābunt.')

2 Further examples:

1 audiō trēs Virginēs Vestālēs damnātās esse.
2 ancilla dīcit dominum in hortō ambulāre.
3 spērāmus ducem auxilium mox missūrum esse.
4 nūntius affirmat Agricolam ad ultimās partēs Britanniae pervēnisse.
5 fēmina putat marītum in illō carcere tenērī.

3 Compare the following examples:

1 Salvius dīcit sē in Ītaliā habitāre.
   (Direct statement: 'in Ītaliā habitō.')
2 ꜱ vius dīcit eum in forō ambulāre.
   (Direct statement: 'in forō ambulat.')

4 The indirect statements in paragraphs 1-3 are each introduced by a verb in the *present* tense (e.g. 'puto', 'crēdit', etc.) Examples introduced by a verb in the *perfect* or *imperfect* tense (e.g. 'putāvī', 'crēdēbat', etc.) are given on pp.110–11, Stage 40.

Gerundives

1 From Stage 24 onwards, you have met the gerundive used in sentences like these:

mihi manendum est.	I must stay.
Haterius culpandus est.	Haterius ought to be blamed.
dea nōbīs laudanda est.	We ought to praise the goddess.
tibi festīnandum erit.	You will have to hurry.
exīstimō Agricolam dēmovendum esse.	I think that Agricola ought to be dismissed.

2 Further examples:
   1 nōbīs in hāc vīllā dormiendum erit.
   2 mihi multae epistulae scrībendae sunt.
   3 exīstimō captīvōs līberandōs esse.

3 A different way of using the gerundive is described on p.115.

Sentences with 'dum' (meaning 'while')

1 From Stage 29 onwards, you have met 'dum' used with the meaning 'while':

dum cīvēs sacrificium spectant, iuvenis subitō prōsiluit.
While the citizens were watching the sacrifice, a young man suddenly leapt forward.

dum bellum in Britanniā geritur, rēs dīra Rōmae accidit.
While the war was being waged in Britain, a terrible disaster happened at Rome.

Notice that in sentences like these 'dum' is used with the indicative *present* tense, even when the statement refers to the past.

Further examples:
1 dum custōdēs dormiunt, captīvī effūgērunt.
2 dum nūntius in līmine haesitat, Imperātor 'intrā!' clāmāvit.

2 For examples of 'dum' used with the meaning 'until', see paragraph 6 on p.151.

PART THREE: VOCABULARY (words and phrases)

Notes

1   Nouns, adjectives, verbs and prepositions are listed as in the Unit IIIB Language Information pamphlet.

2   Verbs like 'crēdō', 'obstō', etc., which are often used with a noun or pronoun in the *dative* case, are marked + *dat*.

Notice again how such verbs are used:

tibi crēdō.
turba nōbīs obstābat.

I put trust in you. *Or,* I trust you.
The crowd was a hindrance to us.
Or, The crowd hindered us.

3   The *present* tense of *second* conjugation verbs like 'doceō' has the same endings (except in the 1st person singular) as the *future* tense of *third* and *fourth* conjugation verbs like 'trahō', 'capiō' and 'audiō': '-ēs', '-et', etc. in the active, and '-ēris', '-ētur', etc. in the passive. Pages 156-83 can be used to check which conjugation a verb belongs to, and thus translate its tense properly.

For example, the conjugation and tense of 'iubent' can be checked in the following way:

The verb is listed on p.169 as 'iubeō, iubēre', etc., so it belongs to the second conjugation like 'doceō, docēre', etc., and therefore 'iubent' must be in the present tense: 'they order'.

And the conjugation and tense of 'dūcent' can be checked like this:

The verb is listed on p.164 as 'dūcō, dūcere', etc., so it belongs to the third conjugation like 'trahō, trahere', etc., and therefore 'dūcent' must be in the future tense: 'they will lead'.

Translate the following words, using pages 156-83 to check conjugation and tense:

1 rīdēs, intellegēs
2 pendent, venient
3 gaudēmus, monēmus

4 convertet, ignōscet
5 prohibentur, regentur
6 dūcēris, iubēris

4   All words which are given in the vocabulary checklists for Stages 1-40 are marked with an asterisk.

a

A. = Aulus

*ā, ab + *abl.* – from; by

abdūcō, abdūcere, abdūxī, abductus – lead away

* abeō, abīre, abiī – go away

abnuō, abnuere, abnuī – refuse

abripiō, abripere, abripuī, abreptus – tear away from

abstineō, abstinēre, abstinuī – abstain

* absum, abesse, āfuī – be out, be absent, be away

absurdus, absurda, absurdum – absurd

* ac – and
    idem . . . ac – the same . . . as

* accidō, accidere, accidī – happen

* accipiō, accipere, accēpī, acceptus – accept, take in, receive

accurrō, accurrere, accurrī – run up

accūsātiō, accūsātiōnis, f. – accusation

accūsātor, accūsātōris, m. – accuser, prosecutor

* accūsō, accūsāre, accūsāvī, accūsātus – accuse

* ācriter – keenly, eagerly, fiercely

* ad + *acc.* – to, at

* addō, addere, addidī, additus – add

addūcō, addūcere, addūxī, adductus – lead, lead on, encourage

* adeō, adīre, adiī – approach, go up to

* adeō – so much, so greatly

adeptus *see* adipīscor

adest *see* adsum

adfīnis, adfīnis, m. – relative, relation by marriage

adfīnitās, adfīnitātis, f. – relationship

* adhūc – up till now

* adipīscor, adipīscī, adeptus sum – receive, obtain

* aditus, aditūs, m. – entrance

adiūtor, adiūtōris, m. – helper

* adiuvō, adiuvāre, adiūvī – help

* administrō, administrāre, administrāvī, administrātus – look after, manage

admoneō, admonēre, admonuī, admonitus – warn, advise

* adstō, adstāre, adstitī – stand by

* adsum, adesse, adfuī – be here, be present

adsūmō, adsūmere, adsūmpsī, adsūmptus – adopt

adulātiō, adulātiōnis, f. – flattery

adulor, adulārī, adulātus sum – flatter

aduncus, adunca, aduncum – curved

* adveniō, advenīre, advēnī – arrive

* adventus, adventūs, m. – arrival

* adversus, adversa, adversum – hostile, unfavorable

*   rēs adversae – misfortune

* adversus + *acc.* – against

advesperāscit, advesperāscere, advesperāvit – get dark, become dark

* aedificium, aedificiī, n. – building

* aedificō, aedificāre, aedificāvī, aedificātus – build

* aeger, aegra, aegrum – sick, ill

Aeolius, Aeolia, Aeolium – Aeolian

* aequus, aequa, aequum – fair, calm

*   aequō animō – calmly, in a calm spirit

aerārium, aerāriī, m. – treasury

aestās, aestātis, f. – summer

aetās, aetātis, f. – age
    aetāte flōrēre – be in the prime of life

aethēr, aetheris, m. – sky, heaven

afferō, afferre, attulī, adlātus – bring

* afficiō, afficere, affēcī, affectus – affect, treat

* affirmō, affirmāre, affirmāvī – declare

afflīgō, afflīgere, afflīxī, afflīctus – afflict, hurt

* ager, agrī, m. – field

* agitō, agitārc, agitāvī, agitātus –
     chase, hunt
* agmen, agminis, n. – column (of
     men), procession
* agnōscō, agnōscere, agnōvī, agnitus –
     recognize
* agō, agere, ēgī, āctus – do, act
*   fābulam agere – act in a play
*   grātiās agere – thank, give thanks
*   negōtium agere – do business, work
     officium agere – do one's duty
     quid agis? – how are you? how are
        you doing?
     triumphum agere – celebrate a
        triumph
     vītam agere – lead a life
* agricola, agricolae, m. – farmer
  āla, ālae, f. – wing
  alacriter – eagerly
* aliquandō – sometimes
  aliquī, aliqua, aliquod – some
* aliquis, aliquid – someone, something
* alius, alia, aliud – other, another, else
     aliī alia – some . . . one thing, some
        . . . another, different people
        . . . different things
*   aliī . . . aliī – some . . . others
* alter, altera, alterum – the other,
     another, the second
     alter . . . alter – one . . . the other
* altus, alta, altum – high, deep
* ambō, ambae, ambō – both
* ambulō, ambulāre, ambulāvī – walk
* amīcitia, amīcitiae, f. – friendship
* amīcus, amīcī, m. – friend
  amīcus, amīca, amīcum – friendly
* āmittō, āmittere, āmīsī, āmissus –
     lose
* amō, amāre, amāvī, amātus – love,
     like
* amor, amōris, m. – love
  amphitheātrum, amphitheātrī, n. –
     amphitheater
* amplector, amplectī, amplexus sum –
     embrace
* amplius – more fully, at greater
     length

* amplissimus, amplissima,
     amplissimum – very great
* an – or
*   utrum . . . an – whether . . . or
* ancilla, ancillae, f. – slave-girl or
     -woman
  angulus, angulī, m. – corner
* angustus, angusta, angustum –
     narrow
  anima, animae, f. – soul, spirit
* animadvertō, animadvertere,
     animadvertī, animadversus –
     notice, take notice of
* animus, animī, m. – spirit, soul, mind
*   aequō animō – calmly, in a calm
        spirit
*   in animō volvere – wonder, turn
        over in the mind
* annus, annī, m. – year
* ante + acc. – before, in front of
* anteā – before
  antidotum, antidotī, n. – antidote,
     remedy
* antīquus, antīqua, antīquum – old,
     ancient
  antrum, antrī, n. – cave
* ānulus, ānulī, m. – ring
  anxius, anxia, anxium – anxious
  aper, aprī, m. – boar
* aperiō, aperīre, aperuī, apertus – open
* appāreō, appārēre, appāruī – appear
* appellō, appellāre, appellāvī,
     appellātus – call, call out to
* appropinquō, appropinquāre,
     appropinquāvī + dat. –
     approach, come near to
* aptus, apta, aptum – suitable
* apud + acc. – among, at the house of
* aqua, aquae, f. – water
  Aquae Sūlis, Aquārum Sūlis, f. pl. –
     Bath (city in England)
  Aquilō, Aquilōnis, m. – North wind
* āra, ārae, f. – altar
* arbor, arboris, f. – tree
* arcessō, arcessere, arcessīvī,
     arcessītus – summon, send for
  ardenter – passionately

* ardeō, ardēre, arsī – burn, be on fire
  ardēscō, ardēscere, arsī – catch fire,
      blaze up
* argenteus, argentea, argenteum –
      made of silver
* arma, armōrum, n. pl. – arms,
      weapons
  armātus, armāta, armātum – armed
  arō, arāre, arāvī, arātus – plow
  arripiō, arripere, arripuī, arreptus –
      seize
* arrogantia, arrogantiae, f. – cheek,
      arrogance
* ars, artis, f. – art, skill
* ascendō, ascendere, ascendī – climb,
      rise
  ascīscō, ascīscere, ascīvī – adopt
  asinus, asinī, m. – donkey
  aspiciō, aspicere, aspexī – look
      towards
  assiduē – continually
* at – but
  āthlēta, āthlētae, m. – athlete
* atque – and
* ātrium, ātriī, n. – atrium, entrance
      room, hall
* attonitus, attonita, attonitum –
      astonished
  attulī see afferō
* auctor, auctōris, m. – creator,
      originator, person responsible
      Salviō auctōre – at Salvius'
      suggestion
* auctōritās, auctōritātis, f. – authority
  auctus see augēre
* audācia, audāciae, f. – boldness,
      audacity
* audāx, gen. audācis – bold, daring
* audeō, audēre – dare
* audiō, audīre, audīvī, audītus – hear
  audītor, audītōris, m. – listener, (pl.)
      audience
  audītōrium, audītōriī, n. – auditorium,
      hall (used for public readings)
* auferō, auferre, abstulī, ablātus –
      take away, steal
* augeō, augēre, auxī, auctus – increase

* aula, aulae, f. – palace
* aureus, aurea, aureum – golden,
      made of gold
  aurīga, aurīgae, m. – charioteer
* auris, auris, f. – ear
* aurum, aurī, n. – gold
* aut – or
* autem – but
  auxiliāris, auxiliāre – additional
* auxilium, auxiliī, n. – help
*   auxiliō esse – be a help, be helpful
* avārus, avārī, m. – miser
  āvertō, āvertere, āvertī, āversus –
      avert, turn away
* avidē – eagerly
* avis, avis, f. – bird
  avus, avī, m. – grandfather
  axis, axis, m. – (arched) vault of
      heaven

b

  balneum, balneī, n. – bath
  barba, barbae, f. – beard
  barbarus, barbara, barbarum –
      barbarian
* barbarus, barbarī, m. – barbarian
  basilica, basilicae, f. – law court
* bellum, bellī, n. – war
*   bellum gerere – wage war,
      campaign
  bellus, bella, bellum – pretty
* bene – well
*   optimē – very well
* beneficium, beneficiī, n. – act of
      kindness, favor
* benignus, benigna, benignum – kind
  bēstia, bēstiae, f. – wild animal, beast
* bibō, bibere, bibī – drink
  bis – twice
* bonus, bona, bonum – good
  bona, bonōrum, n. pl. – goods,
      property
*   melior, melius – better
  melius est – it would be better

* optimus, optima, optimum – very good, excellent, best
* bracchium, bracchiī, n. – arm
* brevis, breve – short, brief
  breviter – briefly
  Britannī, Britannōrum, m.pl. – Britons
  Britannia, Britanniae, f. – Britain

C

C. = Gāius
cachinnō, cachinnāre, cachinnāvī – laugh, cackle
* cadō, cadere, cecidī – fall
* caedō, caedere, cecīdī, caesus – kill
* caelum, caelī, n. – sky, heaven
  caeruleus, caerulea, caeruleum – blue, from the deep blue sea
  Calēdonia, Calēdoniae, f. – Scotland
  Calēdoniī, Calēdoniōrum, m.pl – Caledonians (Scottish tribespeople)
* callidus, callida, callidum – clever, cunning, shrewd
* campus, campī, m. – plain
* canis, canis, m. – dog
* cantō, cantāre, cantāvī – sing, chant
  cānus, cāna, cānum – white
  capella, capellae, f. – she-goat
* capillī, capillōrum, m.pl – hair
* capiō, capere, cēpī, captus – take, catch, capture
* captīvus, captīvī, m. – prisoner, captive
  captō, captāre, captāvī, captātus – try to catch
* caput, capitis, n. – head
* carcer, carceris, m. – prison
* carmen, carminis, n. – song
  carnifex, carnificis, m. – executioner
  carpō, carpere, carpsī, carptus – pluck, seize, crop
* cārus, cāra, cārum – dear
  casa, casae, f. – small house, cottage
* castīgō, castīgāre, castīgāvī, castīgātus – scold

* castra, castrōrum, n.pl. – camp
* cāsus, cāsūs, m. – misfortune
* catēna, catēnae, f. – chain
* causa, causae, f. – reason, cause; case (of law)
  causam dīcere – plead a case
* cautē – cautiously
* caveō, cavēre, cāvī – beware
  caverna, cavernae, f. – cave, cavern
* cēdō, cēdere, cessī – give in, yield
* celebrō, celebrāre, celebrāvī, celebrātus – celebrate
* celeriter – quickly, fast
  quam celerrimē – as quickly as possible
* cēlō, cēlāre, cēlāvī, cēlātus – hide
* cēna, cēnae, f. – dinner
* cēnō, cēnāre, cēnāvī – dine, have dinner
* centum – a hundred
* centuriō, centuriōnis, m. – centurion
* cēra, cērae, f. – wax, wax tablet
* certāmen, certāminis, n. – struggle, fight
  certē – certainly
* certō, certāre, certāvī – compete
* certus, certa, certum – certain, infallible
*   prō certō habēre – know for certain
* cēterī, cēterae, cētera – the others, the rest
  chorus, chorī, m. – chorus, choir
* cibus, cibī, m. – food
* cinis, cineris, m. – ash
* circum + acc. – around
  circumeō, circumīre, circumiī – go round, go around
* circumspectō, circumspectāre, circumspectāvī – look round
* circumveniō, circumvenīre, circumvēnī, circumventus – surround
  circus, circī, m. – circus, stadium
* cīvis, cīvis, m.f. – citizen
* clam – secretly, in private
* clāmō, clāmāre, clāmāvī – shout
* clāmor, clāmōris, m. – shout, uproar

* clārus, clāra, clārum – famous, distinguished, splendid
* claudō, claudere, clausī, clausus – shut, close, block, conclude
* cliēns, clientis, m. – client
cloāca, cloācae, f. – drain
Cn. = Gnaeus
coāctus *see* cōgō
* coepī – I began
* cōgitō, cōgitāre, cōgitāvī – think, consider
cognāta, cognātae, f. – relative (by birth)
cognitiō, cognitiōnis, f. – trial
    cognitiō senātūs – trial by the senate
cognōmen, cognōminis, n. – surname, additional name
* cognōscō, cognōscere, cognōvī, cognitus – get to know, find out
* cōgō, cōgere, coēgī, coāctus – force, compel
* cohors, cohortis, f. – cohort
* colligō, colligere, collēgī, collēctus – gather, collect, assemble
collis, collis, m. – hill
* collocō, collocāre, collocāvī, collocātus – place, put
* colloquium, colloquiī, n. – talk, chat
colloquor, colloquī, collocūtus sum – talk, chat
colōnus, colōnī, m. – tenant-farmer
* comes, comitis, m.f. – comrade, companion
cōmiter – politely, courteously
* comitor, comitārī, comitātus sum – accompany
* commemorō, commemorāre, commemorāvī, commemorātus – talk about, mention, recall
* commendō, commendāre, commendāvī, commendātus – recommend
committō, committere, commīsī, commissus – commit, begin
commodē – appropriately

* commodus, commoda, commodum – convenient
* commōtus, commōta, commōtum – moved, upset, affected, alarmed, excited, distressed, overcome
* comparō, comparāre, comparāvī, comparātus – (1) obtain
    (2) compare
* compleō, complēre, complēvī, complētus – fill
* complūrēs, complūra – several
* compōnō, compōnere, composuī, compositus – put together, arrange, settle, mix, compose, make up
    compositus, composita, compositum – composed, steady
* comprehendō, comprehendere, comprehendī, comprehēnsus – arrest, seize
cōnātur *see* cōnor
concavus, concava, concavum – hollow
concipiō, concipere, concēpī, conceptus – take
    concipere flammās – burst into flames
* condūcō, condūcere, condūxī, conductus – hire
cōnfarreātiō, cōnfarreātiōnis, f. – marriage ceremony
* cōnficiō, cōnficere, cōnfēcī, cōnfectus – finish
* cōnfectus, cōnfecta, cōnfectum – worn out, exhausted, overcome
* cōnfīdō, cōnfīdere + *dat.* – trust, put trust; be sure, be confident
cōnfīgō, cōnfīgere, cōnfīxī, cōnfīxus – stab, skewer
* coniciō, conicere, coniēcī, coniectus – hurl, throw
* coniūnx, coniugis, f. – wife
* coniūrātiō, coniūrātiōnis, f. – plot, conspiracy
* cōnor, cōnārī, cōnātus sum – try

* cōnscendō, cōnscendere, cōnscendī –
    climb on, embark on, go on
    board, mount
cōnscīscō, cōnscīscere, cōnscīvī –
    inflict
    mortem sibi cōnscīscere – commit
        suicide
cōnsecrō, cōnsecrāre, cōnsecrāvī,
    cōnsecrātus – dedicate
* cōnsentiō, cōnsentīre, cōnsēnsī –
    agree
cōnsīderātus, cōnsīderāta,
    cōnsīderātum – careful,
    well-considered
cōnsīdō, cōnsīdere, cōnsēdī – sit down
* cōnsilium, cōnsiliī, n. – plan, idea,
    advice; council
* cōnsistō, cōnsistere, cōnstitī –
    stand one's ground, stand firm,
    halt, stop
cōnsōlor, cōnsōlārī, cōnsōlātus
    sum – console
* cōnspiciō, cōnspicere, cōnspexī,
    cōnspectus – catch sight of
* cōnspicor, cōnspicārī, cōnspicātus
    sum – catch sight of
cōnstat, cōnstāre, cōnstitit – be agreed
*   satis cōnstat – it is generally agreed
* cōnstituō, cōnstituere, cōnstituī,
    cōnstitūtus – decide
* cōnsul, cōnsulis, m. – consul (highest
    elected official of Roman
    government)
cōnsulāris, cōnsulāris, m. – ex-consul
* cōnsulātus, cōnsulātūs, m. – the office
    of consul
* cōnsulō, cōnsulere, cōnsuluī,
    cōnsultus – consult
* cōnsūmō, cōnsūmere, cōnsūmpsī,
    cōnsūmptus – eat
* contendō, contendere, contendī –
    hurry
* contentus, contenta, contentum –
    satisfied
contineō, continēre, continuī –
    contain

contingō, contingere, contigī,
    contāctus – touch
continuus, continua, continuum –
    continuous, on end
* contrā + acc. – against
contrahō, contrahere, contrāxī,
    contractus – draw together
    supercilia contrahere – draw
        eyebrows together, frown
contumēlia, contumēliae, f. – insult,
    abuse
convalēscō, convalēscere, convaluī –
    get better, recover
* conveniō, convenīre, convēnī –
    come together, gather, meet
    in manum convenīre – pass into the
        hands of
* convertō, convertere, convertī,
    conversus – turn
    sē convertere – turn
convertor, convertī, conversus sum –
    turn
* cōpiae, cōpiārum, f.pl. – forces
* coquō, coquere, coxī, coctus – cook
* coquus, coquī, m. – cook
* corōna, corōnae, f. – garland, wreath
* corpus, corporis, n. – body
corrumpō, corrumpere, corrūpī,
    corruptus – corrupt
* cotīdiē – every day
* crās – tomorrow
crāstinus, crāstina, crāstinum –
    tomorrow's
* crēdō, crēdere, crēdidī + dat. –
    trust, believe, have faith in
cremō, cremāre, cremāvī, cremātus –
    cremate, burn, destroy by fire
* creō, creāre, creāvī, creātus – make,
    create
* crīmen, crīminis, n. – charge
* crūdēlis, crūdēle – cruel
crūdēliter – cruelly
* cubiculum, cubiculī, n. – bedroom
cuiuscumque see quīcumque
culmen, culminis, n. – roof
* culpō, culpāre, culpāvī – blame

* cum (1) – when
   cum prīmum – as soon as
* cum (2) + *abl.* – with
  cumba, cumbae, f. – boat
  cūnctanter – slowly, hesitantly
  cupīdō, cupīdinis, f. – desire
* cupiō, cupere, cupīvī – want
* cūr? – why?
* cūra, cūrae, f. – care
*   cūrae esse – be a matter of concern
* cūria, cūriae, f. – senate-house
* cūrō, cūrāre, cūrāvī – look after,
     supervise
   nihil cūrō – I don't care
* currō, currere, cucurrī – run
* cursus, cursūs, m. – course, flight
* custōdiō, custōdīre, custōdīvī,
     custōdītus – guard
* custōs, custōdis, m. – guard

d

  damnātiō, damnātiōnis, f. –
     condemnation
* damnō, damnāre, damnāvī,
     damnātus – condemn
  datus *see* dō
* dē + *abl.* – from, down from; about,
    over
* dea, deae, f. – goddess
* dēbeō, dēbēre, dēbuī, dēbitus – owe;
    ought, should, must
* decem – ten
  dēcernō, dēcernere, dēcrēvī,
    dēcrētus – vote, decree
* decet, decēre, decuit – be proper
   nōs decet – we ought
* dēcidō, dēcidere, dēcidī – fall down
* decimus, decima, decimum – tenth
* dēcipiō, dēcipere, dēcēpī, dēceptus –
    deceive, trick
* decōrus, decōra, decōrum – right,
    proper
  dedī *see* dō
  dēdō, dēdere, dēdidī, dēditus – give
    up

  sē dēdere – surrender, give oneself
    up
  dēdūcō, dēdūcere, dēdūxī, dēductus –
    escort
  dēeram *see* dēsum
* dēfendō, dēfendere, dēfendī, dēfēnsus
    – defend
  dēfēnsiō, dēfēnsiōnis, f. – defense
* dēfessus, dēfessa, dēfessum –
    exhausted, tired out
  dēficiō, dēficere, dēfēcī – fail, die
    away
  dēfīgō, dēfīgere, dēfīxī, dēfīxus – fix
  dēfīxiō, dēfīxiōnis, f. – curse
  dēfōrmis, dēfōrme – ugly, inelegant
* dēiciō, dēicere, dēiēcī, dēiectus –
    throw down, throw
  dēiectus, dēiecta, dēiectum –
    disappointed, downcast
* deinde – then
* dēlectō, dēlectāre, dēlectāvī,
    dēlectātus – delight, please
* dēleō, dēlēre, dēlēvī, dēlētus – destroy
  dēliciae, dēliciārum, f.pl. – darling
  dēligō, dēligāre, dēligāvī,
    dēligātus – bind, tie, tie up, moor
* dēmittō, dēmittere, dēmīsī,
    dēmissus – let down, lower
* dēmōnstrō, dēmōnstrāre,
    dēmōnstrāvī, dēmōnstrātus –
    point out, show
* dēmum – at last
*   tum dēmum – then at last, only
    then
* dēnique – at last, finally
  dēns, dentis, m. – tooth, tusk
* dēnsus, dēnsa, dēnsum – thick
* dēpōnō, dēpōnere, dēposuī,
    dēpositus – put down, take off
  dēprehendō, dēprehendere,
    dēprehendī, dēprehēnsus –
    discover
  dēprendō = dēprehendō
* dērīdeō, dērīdēre, dērīsī, dērīsus –
    mock, make fun of
  dēripiō, dēripere, dēripuī,
    dēreptus – tear down

* dēscendō, dēscendere, dēscendī – go down, come down
* dēserō, dēserere, dēseruī, dēsertus – desert
* dēsiliō, dēsilīre, dēsiluī – jump down
* dēsinō, dēsinere – end, cease
  dēsistō, dēsistere, dēstitī – stop
  dēspērātiō, dēspērātiōnis, f. – despair
* dēspērō, dēspērāre, dēspērāvī – despair, give up
  dēsum, dēesse, dēfuī – be lacking, be missing
* deus, deī, m. – god
*   dī immortālēs! – heavens above!
  dī inferī – gods of the Underworld
* dextra, dextrae, f. – right hand
* dīcō, dīcere, dīxī, dictus – say
  causam dīcere – plead a case
  dictus, dicta, dictum – appointed
* dictō, dictāre, dictāvī, dictātus – dictate
  didicī see discō
* diēs, diēī, m. f. – day
*   diēs nātālis, diēī nātālis, m. – birthday
* difficilis, difficile – difficult
* dignitās, dignitātis, f. – dignity, importance, honor, prestige
* dignus, digna, dignum – worthy, appropriate
* dīligenter – carefully
* dīligentia, dīligentiae, f. – industry, hard work
* dīligō, dīligere, dīlēxī – be fond of
  dīluvium, dīluviī, n. – flood
* dīmittō, dīmittere, dīmīsī, dīmissus – send away, dismiss
* dīrus, dīra, dīrum – dreadful
  dīs see deus
* discēdō, discēdere, discessī – depart, leave
* discipulus, discipulī, m. – disciple, follower, pupil, student
* discō, discere, didicī – learn
* discrīmen, discrīminis, n. – boundary, dividing line; crisis

displiceō, displicēre, displicuī + *dat.* – displease
* dissentiō, dissentīre, dissēnsī – disagree, argue
  dissimulō, dissimulāre, dissimulāvī, dissimulātus – conceal, hide
  distrahō, distrahere, distrāxī, distractus – tear apart, tear in two
  distribuō, distribuere, distribuī, distribūtus – distribute
* diū – for a long time
  dīversus, dīversa, dīversum – different
* dīves, *gen.* dīvitis – rich
* dīvitiae, dīvitiārum, f.pl. – riches
* dīvus, dīvī, m. – god
  dīxī see dīcō
* dō, dare, dedī, datus – give
*   poenās dare – pay the penalty, be punished
* doceō, docēre, docuī, doctus – teach
*   doctus, docta, doctum – learned, educated, skillful, clever
* doleō, dolēre, doluī – hurt, be in pain; grieve, be sad
* dolor, dolōris, m. – pain, grief
* domina, dominae, f. – lady (of the house), mistress
* dominus, dominī, m. – master (of the house)
* domus, domūs, f. – home
  domī – at home
  domum Hateriī – to Haterius' house
  domum redīre – return home
* dōnō, dōnāre, dōnāvī, dōnātus – give
* dōnum, dōnī, n. – present, gift
* dormiō, dormīre, dormīvī – sleep
* dubitō, dubitāre, dubitāvī – hesitate, doubt
  nōn dubitō quīn – I do not doubt that
* dubium, dubiī, n. – doubt
  ducem see dux
* ducentī, ducentae, ducenta – two hundred

* dūcō, dūcere, dūxī, ductus – lead
  uxōrem dūcere – take as a wife,
  marry
* dulcis, dulce – sweet
* dum – while, until, so long as
* duo, duae, duo – two
* duodecim – twelve
* duodēvīgintī – eighteen
* dūrus, dūra, dūrum – harsh, hard
* dux, ducis, m. – leader
  dūxī *see* dūcō

e

* ē, ex + *abl.* – from, out of
  eandem *see* īdem
* ecce! – see! look!
  efferō, efferre, extulī, ēlātus – bring
  out, carry out
    ēlātus, ēlāta, ēlātum – thrilled,
    excited, carried away
* efficiō, efficere, effēcī, effectus – carry
  out, accomplish
* effigiēs, effigiēī, f. – image, statue
* effugiō, effugere, effūgī – escape
* effundō, effundere, effūdī, effūsus –
  pour out
  ēgī *see* agō
* ego, meī – I, me
  mēcum – with me
* ēgredior, ēgredī, ēgressus sum – go
  out
* ēheu! – alas! o dear!
* ēiciō, ēicere, ēiēcī, ēiectus – throw out
  eīdem *see* īdem
  ēlābor, ēlābī, ēlāpsus sum – escape
  ēlātus *see* efferō
  ēlegāns, *gen.* ēlegantis – tasteful,
  elegant
* ēligō, ēligere, ēlēgī, ēlēctus – choose
* ēmittō, ēmittere, ēmīsī, ēmissus –
  throw, send out
* emō, emere, ēmī, ēmptus – buy
  ēn! – look!
* enim – for
* eō, īre, iī – go

* obviam īre + *dat.* – meet, go to meet
  eōdem, eōsdem *see* īdem
  epigramma, epigrammatis, n. –
  epigram
* epistula, epistulae, f. – letter
* eques, equitis, m. – horseman; man of
  equestrian rank
  equidem – indeed
* equitō, equitāre, equitāvī – ride
  (a horse)
* equus, equī, m. – horse
  ērādō, ērādere, ērāsī, ērāsus – erase
  eram *see* sum
* ergō – therefore
* ēripiō, ēripere, ēripuī, ēreptus –
  snatch, tear, rescue, snatch away
* errō, errāre, errāvī – make a mistake;
  wander
  longē errāre – make a big mistake
  ērubēscō, ērubēscere, ērubuī – blush
  ērumpō, ērumpere, ērūpī – break
  away, break out
  est, estō *see* sum
* et – and
*   et . . . et – both . . . and
* etiam – even, also
  nōn modo . . . sed etiam – not only
  . . . but also
* euge! – hurrah!
  ēvolō, ēvolāre, ēvolāvī – fly out
  ēvolvō, ēvolvere, ēvolvī, ēvolūtus –
  unroll, open
  ēvomō, ēvomere, ēvomuī, ēvomitus –
  spit out, spew out
* ex, ē + *abl.* – from, out of
* exanimātus, exanimāta, exanimātum
  – unconscious
* excipiō, excipere, excēpī, exceptus –
  receive, take over
* excitō, excitāre, excitāvī, excitātus –
  arouse, wake up, awaken
* exclāmō, exclāmāre, exclāmāvī –
  exclaim, shout
  excōgitō, excōgitāre, excōgitāvī,
  excōgitātus – invent, think up
  excruciō, excruciāre, excruciāvī,
  excruciātus – torture, torment

* exemplum, exemplī, n. – example
* exeō, exīre, exiī – go out
* exerceō, exercēre, exercuī,
 exercitus – exercise, practise,
 train
* exercitus, exercitūs, m. – army
 exigō, exigere, exēgī, exāctus –
 demand
* exilium, exiliī, n. – exile
* exīstimō, exīstimāre, exīstimāvī,
 exīstimātus – think, consider
* exitium, exitiī, n. – ruin,
 destruction
* explicō, explicāre, explicāvī,
 explicātus – explain
 explōrātor, explōrātōris, m. –
 scout, spy
 expōnō, expōnere, exposuī,
 expositus – unload; set out,
 explain
 exspatior, exspatiārī, exspatiātus
 sum – extend, spread out
* exspectō, exspectāre, exspectāvī,
 exspectātus – wait for
* exstinguō, exstinguere, exstīnxī,
 exstīnctus – extinguish, put out,
 destroy
* exstruō, exstruere, exstrūxī,
 exstrūctus – build
 exsultō, exsultāre, exsultāvī –
 exult, be triumphant
 extendō, extendere, extendī,
 extentus – stretch out
* extrā + acc. – outside
* extrahō, extrahere, extrāxī,
 extractus – drag out, pull out,
 take out
* extrēmus, extrēma, extrēmum –
 furthest
 extrēma scaena – the edge of the
 stage

f

* faber, fabrī, m. – craftsman,
 carpenter, workman

* fābula, fābulae, f. – play, story
* fābulam agere – act in a play
 fābulōsus, fābulōsa, fābulōsum –
 legendary, famous
 facēs see fax
 faciēs, faciēī, f. – face
* facile – easily
* facilis, facile – easy
* facinus, facinoris, n. – crime
* faciō, facere, fēcī, factus – make, do
 floccī nōn faciō – I don't care a
 hang for
 quid faciam? – what am I to do?
 fācundē – fluently, eloquently
 fācundus, fācunda, fācundum –
 fluent, eloquent
* fallō, fallere, fefellī, falsus – deceive,
 escape notice of, slip by
 falsum, falsī, n. – lie, forgery
* falsus, falsa, falsum – false, untrue,
 dishonest
* fāma, fāmae, f. – rumor
* familia, familiae, f. – household
* familiāris, familiāris, m. – close
 friend, relation, relative
 farreus, farrea, farreum – made from
 grain
 fascinātiō, fascinātiōnis, f. – the evil
 eye
 Fāstī, Fāstōrum, m.pl. – the list of the
 consuls
* faveō, favēre, fāvī + dat. – favor,
 support
* favor, favōris, m. – favor
* fax, facis, f. – torch
 febris, febris, m. – fever
 fēcī see faciō
 fēlīciter! – good luck!
* fēmina, fēminae, f. – woman
 fenestra, fenestrae, f. – window
* ferō, ferre, tulī, lātus – bring, carry
* ferōciter – fiercely
* ferōx, gen. ferōcis – fierce, ferocious
* ferrum, ferrī, n. – iron, sword
* fessus, fessa, fessum – tired
* festīnō, festīnāre, festīnāvī – hurry
* fēstus, fēsta, fēstum – festival, holiday

* fidēlis, fidēle – faithful, loyal
* fidēs, fideī, f. – loyalty, trust-
    worthiness
* filia, filiae, f. – daughter
* filius, filiī, m. – son
* fingō, fingere, finxī, fictus – pretend,
    invent, forge
* finis, finis, m. – end
* fiō, fierī, factus sum – become, be
    made, occur
  firmē – firmly
  firmō, firmāre, firmāvī, firmātus –
    strengthen, establish
  firmus, firma, firmum – firm
* flamma, flammae, f. – flame
    concipere flammās – burst into
    flames
  flammeum, flammeī, n. – veil
  floccī nōn faciō – I don't care a hang
    for
* flōreō, flōrēre, flōruī – flourish
    aetāte flōrēre – be in the prime of
    life
* flōs, flōris, m. – flower
* flūmen, flūminis, n. – river
* fluō, fluere, flūxī – flow
  foedus, foeda, foedum – foul, horrible
* fōns, fontis, m. – fountain, spring
  forās – out of the house
* fortasse – perhaps
* forte – by chance
* fortis, forte – brave
* fortiter – bravely
* fortūna, fortūnae, f. – fortune, luck
  fortūnātus, fortūnāta, fortūnātum –
    lucky
* forum, forī, n. – forum, business
    center
* fossa, fossae, f. – ditch
* fragor, fragōris, m. – crash
* frangō, frangere, frēgī, frāctus – break
* frāter, frātris, m. – brother
* fraus, fraudis, f. – trick
* frūmentum, frūmentī, n. – grain
  fruor, fruī, fructus sum – enjoy
* frūstrā – in vain
* fuga, fugae, f. – escape

* fugiō, fugere, fūgī – run away, flee
    (from)
  fugitīvus, fugitīvī, m. – fugitive,
    runaway
  fuī see sum
* fulgeō, fulgēre, fulsī – shine, glitter
  fulmen, fulminis, n. – thunderbolt
  fulvus, fulva, fulvum – tawny
* fundō, fundere, fūdī, fūsus – pour
* fundus, fundī, m. – farm
* fūr, fūris, m. – thief
* furēns, *gen.* furentis – furious, in a
    rage
  futūrus see sum

g

* gaudeō, gaudēre – be pleased, rejoice
* gaudium, gaudiī, n. – joy
  gelō, gelāre, gelāvī, gelātus – freeze
* geminī, geminōrum, m.pl. – twins
* gemitus, gemitūs, m. – groan
* gemma, gemmae, f. – jewel, gem
  gener, generī, m. – son-in-law
* gēns, gentis, f. – family, tribe, race
* genus, generis, n. – race
    genus mortāle – the human race
  Germānī, Germānōrum, m.pl. –
    Germans
  Germānus, Germāna, Germānum –
    German
* gerō, gerere, gessī, gestus – wear;
    achieve
*   bellum gerere – wage war,
    campaign
    sē gerere – behave, conduct oneself
* gladius, gladiī, m. – sword
  glōria, glōriae, f. – glory
  glōriōsus, glōriōsa, glōriōsum –
    boastful
  gracilis, gracile – graceful
  grāmen, grāminis, n. – grass
  grātiae, grātiārum, f.pl. – thanks
*   grātiās agere – thank, give thanks
  grātulātiō, grātulātiōnis, f. –
    congratulation

* grātus, grāta, grātum – acceptable,
    pleasing
* gravis, grave – heavy, serious
* graviter – heavily, soundly, seriously
    gravō, gravāre, gravāvī – load, weigh
    down
* gustō, gustāre, gustāvī – taste

h

* habeō, habēre, habuī, habitus –
    have
*   prō certō habēre – know for certain
* habitō, habitāre, habitāvī – live
* haereō, haerēre, haesī – stick, cling
* haesitō, haesitāre, haesitāvī – hesitate
* haruspex, haruspicis, m. – diviner,
    soothsayer
* hasta, hastae, f. – spear
* haud – not
* haudquāquam – not at all
* hauriō, haurīre, hausī, haustus –
    drain, drink up
* hercle! – by Hercules!
* hērēs, hērēdis, m.f. – heir
* heri – yesterday
    Hibernī, Hibernōrum, m.pl. – Irish
    Hibernia, Hiberniae, f. – Ireland
* hic, haec, hoc – this
        hic . . . ille – this one . . . that one,
        one man . . . another man
* hīc – here
* hiems, hiemis, f. – winter
* hinc – from here; then, next
    Hispānia, Hispāniae, f. – Spain
* hodiē – today
* homō, hominis, m. – person
    homunculus, homunculī, m. – little
    man, pip-squeak
* honor, honōris, m. – honor, official
    position
* honōrō, honōrāre, honōrāvī,
    honōrātus – honor
* hōra, hōrae, f. – hour
    horrendus, horrenda, horrendum –
    horrifying

horrēscō, horrēscere, horruī –
    shudder
* horreum, horreī, n. – barn, granary
* hortor, hortārī, hortātus sum –
    encourage, urge
* hortus, hortī, m. – garden
* hospes, hospitis, m. – guest, host
* hostis, hostis, m.f. – enemy
* hūc – here, to this place
        hūc . . . illūc – this way . . . that
        way, one way . . . another way
    humus, humī, f. – ground
*   humī – on the ground
    Hymēn, Hymenis, m. – Hymen, god
    of weddings
    Hymenaeus, Hymenaeī, m. –
    Hymen, god of weddings

i

* iaceō, iacēre, iacuī – lie, rest
* iaciō, iacere, iēcī, iactus – throw
* iactō, iactāre, iactāvī, iactātus –
    throw
* iam – now
* iānua, iānuae, f. – door
* ibi – there
* īdem, eadem, idem – the same
        idem . . . ac – the same . . . as
* identidem – repeatedly
* ideō – for this reason
*   ideō . . . quod – for the reason that,
        because
* igitur – therefore, and so
* ignārus, ignāra, ignārum – not
        knowing, unaware
* ignāvus, ignāva, ignāvum – lazy,
        cowardly
* ignis, ignis, m. – fire
* ignōrō, ignōrāre, ignōrāvī – not know
        about
* ignōscō, ignōscere, ignōvī + *dat.* –
        forgive
    iī *see* eō

*ille, illa, illud – that, he, she
    hic . . . ille – this one . . . that one,
      one man . . . another man
  illīc – there, in that place
*illūc – there, to that place
    hūc . . . illūc – this way . . . that
      way, one way . . . another way
  illūcēscō, illūcēscere, illūxī – dawn,
    grow bright
  imāgō, imāginis, f. – image, picture,
    bust
  imber, imbris, m. – rain
*immemor, *gen.* immemoris – forgetful
*immineō, imminēre, imminuī + *dat.* –
    hang over
  immō – or rather
*immortālis, immortāle – immortal
*   dī immortālēs! – heavens above!
*immōtus, immōta, immōtum – still,
    motionless
*impediō, impedīre, impedīvī,
    impedītus – delay, hinder
*imperātor, imperātōris, m. –
    emperor
*imperium, imperiī, n. – power,
    empire
*imperō, imperāre, imperāvī + *dat.* –
    order, command
  impetrō, impetrāre, impetrāvī –
    obtain
*impetus, impetūs, m. – attack
  implicō, implicāre, implicāvī,
    implicātus – implicate, involve
*impōnō, impōnere, imposuī,
    impositus – impose, put into, put
    onto
  imprōvīsus, imprōvīsa, imprōvīsum –
    unexpected, unforeseen
  impudentia, impudentiae, f. –
    shamelessness
  impūrus, impūra, impūrum –
    immoral
*in (1) + *acc.* – into, onto
    (2) + *abl.* – in, on
*inānis, ināne – empty, meaningless
*incēdō, incēdere, incessī – march,
    stride

*incendō, incendere, incendī,
    incēnsus – burn, set fire to
*incēnsus, incēnsa, incēnsum –
    inflamed, angered
  incertus, incerta, incertum –
    uncertain
  incestum, incestī, n. – immorality,
    unchastity
*incidō, incidere, incidī – fall
  incīdō, incīdere, incīsī, incīsus – cut
    open
*incipiō, incipere, incēpī, inceptus –
    begin
*incitō, incitāre, incitāvī, incitātus –
    urge on, encourage
  inclūdō, inclūdere, inclūsī, inclūsus –
    shut up
*inde – then
*indicium, indiciī, n. – sign, evidence
  indulgeō, indulgēre, indulsī + *dat.* –
    give way
*induō, induere, induī, indūtus – put
    on
  indūtus, indūta, indūtum – dressed
*īnfāns, īnfantis, m. – baby, child
*īnfēlīx, *gen.* īnfēlīcis – unlucky
*īnferō, īnferre, intulī, inlātus – bring
    in, bring on, bring against
  īnferus, īnfera, īnferum – of the
    Underworld
  dī īnferī – gods of the Underworld
*īnfestus, īnfesta, īnfestum – hostile,
    dangerous
*ingenium, ingeniī, n. – character
*ingēns, *gen.* ingentis – huge
  ingravēscō, ingravēscere – grow
    worse
*ingredior, ingredī, ingressus sum –
    enter
*iniciō, inicere, iniēcī, iniectus – throw
    in
*inimīcus, inimīcī, m. – enemy
*initium, initiī, n. – beginning
*iniūria, iniūriae, f. – injustice, injury
  iniūstē – unfairly
  inlātus *see* īnferō
  innocēns, *gen.* innocentis – innocent

168

innocentia, innocentiae, f. –
    innocence
inquiētus, inquiēta, inquiētum –
    unsettled
*inquit – says, said
īnsānus, īnsāna, īnsānum – insane,
    crazy
īnscrībō, īnscrībere, īnscrīpsī,
    īnscrīptus – write, inscribe
*īnsidiae, īnsidiārum, f.pl. – trap,
    ambush
*īnspiciō, īnspicere, īnspexī,
    īnspectus – look at, inspect,
    examine
īnstō, īnstāre, īnstitī – be pressing,
    threaten
*īnstruō, īnstruere, īnstrūxī,
    īnstrūctus – draw up, set up
    sē īnstruere – draw oneself up
*īnsula, īnsulae, f. – island; apartment
    building
*īnsum, inesse, īnfuī – be in, be inside
*intellegō, intellegere, intellēxī,
    intellēctus – understand
*intentē – intently
*inter + acc. – among
    inter sē – among themselves, with
    each other
*intereā – meanwhile
*interficiō, interficere, interfēcī,
    interfectus – kill
*interim – meanwhile
interpellātiō, interpellātiōnis, f. –
    interruption
interpellō, interpellāre, interpellāvī –
    interrupt
interrogō, interrogāre, interrogāvī,
    interrogātus – question
*intrā + acc. – inside
intremō, intremere, intremuī – shake
*intrō, intrāre, intrāvī – enter
intus – inside
*inveniō, invenīre, invēnī, inventus –
    find
*invideō, invidēre, invīdī, invīsus –
    envy, be jealous of

*invidia, invidiae, f. – jealousy, envy,
    unpopularity
*invītō, invītāre, invītāvī, invītātus –
    invite
*invītus, invīta, invītum – unwilling,
    reluctant
*iocus, iocī, m. – joke
Iovis see Iuppiter
*ipse, ipsa, ipsum – himself, herself,
    itself
*īra, īrae, f. – anger
īrāscor, īrāscī, īrātus sum + dat. –
    become angry with
*īrātus, īrāta, īrātum – angry
īre see eō
*irrumpō, irrumpere, irrūpī – burst in,
    burst into
*is, ea, id – he, she, it
    id quod – what
*iste, ista, istud – that
*ita – in this way
    sīcut . . . ita – just as . . . so
*ita vērō – yes
Ītalia, Ītaliae, f. – Italy
*itaque – and so
*iter, itineris, n. – journey, progress
*iterum – again
*iubeō, iubēre, iussī, iussus – order
*iūdex, iūdicis, m. – judge
iūdicium, iūdiciī, n. – judgement
*iungō, iungere, iūnxī, iūnctus – join
Iūnō, Iūnōnis, f. – Juno (goddess of
    marriage)
Iuppiter, Iovis, m. – Jupiter (god of
    the sky, greatest of Roman gods)
iūrō, iūrāre, iūrāvī – swear
iussī see iubeō
*iussum, iussī, n. – order, instruction
    iussū Imperātōris – at the
    Emperor's order
*iuvenis, iuvenis, m. – young man
*iuvō, iuvāre, iūvī, iūtus – help, assist
iuxtā – side by side

l

L. = Lūcius
* labor, labōris, m. – work
* labōrō, labōrāre, labōrāvī – work
* lacrima, lacrimae, f. – tear
* lacrimō, lacrimāre, lacrimāvī –
    weep, cry
* laedō, laedere, laesī, laesus – harm
    laetē – happily
* laetus, laeta, laetum – happy
    langueō, languēre – feel weak, feel sick
    lassō, lassāre, lassāvī, lassātus – tire,
    weary
* lateō, latēre, latuī – lie hidden
    Latīnus, Latīna, Latīnum – Latin
* latrō, latrōnis, m. – robber
* lātus, lāta, lātum – wide
* laudō, laudāre, laudāvī, laudātus –
    praise
* lavō, lavāre, lāvī, lautus – wash
* lectīca, lectīcae, f. – sedan-chair
* lectus, lectī, m. – couch, bed
* lēgātus, lēgātī, m. – commander
    lēgem see lēx
* legiō, legiōnis, f. – legion
* legō, legere, lēgī, lēctus – read
    lēniō, lēnīre, lēnīvī, lēnītus – soothe,
    calm down
* lēniter – gently
* lentē – slowly
* leō, leōnis, m. – lion
* levis, leve – light, slight, trivial,
    changeable
* lēx, lēgis, f. – law
    libellus, libellī, m. – little book
* libenter – gladly
* liber, librī, m. – book
* līberālis, līberāle – generous
* līberī, līberōrum, m.pl. – children
* līberō, līberāre, līberāvī, līberātus –
    free, set free
* lībertās, lībertātis, f. – freedom
* lībertus, lībertī, m. – freedman,
    ex-slave
    librum see liber
    lībum, lībī, n. – cake

licet, licēre – be allowed
    mihi licet – I am allowed
* līmen, līminis, n. – threshold,
    doorway
* lingua, linguae, f. – tongue
    liquidus, liquida, liquidum – liquid
* littera, litterae, f. – letter (of
    alphabet)
*   litterae, litterārum, f.pl. – letter,
    letters (correspondence),
    literature
* lītus, lītoris, n. – sea-shore, shore
* locus, locī, m. – place
    longē – far
    longē errāre – make a big mistake
* longus, longa, longum – long
* loquor, loquī, locūtus sum – speak
    lūcem see lūx
    lūctor, lūctārī, lūctātus sum –
    struggle
* lūdus, lūdī, m. – game
* lūna, lūnae, f. – moon
    lupus, lupī, m. – wolf
    lūscus, lūsca, lūscum – one-eyed
* lūx, lūcis, f. – light, daylight

m

M. = Marcus
M'. = Mānius
    madidus, madida, madidum – soaked
* magister, magistrī, m. – master,
    foreman
* magnopere – greatly
*   magis – more
*   maximē – very greatly, very much,
    most of all
* magnus, magna, magnum – big,
    large, great
    maior, gen. maiōris – bigger,
    larger, greater
*   maximus, maxima, maximum –
    very big, very large, very great,
    greatest
    Pontifex Maximus – Chief Priest
* male – badly, unfavorably

* mālō, mālle, māluī – prefer
* malus, mala, malum – evil, bad
*   pessimus, pessima, pessimum –
      very bad, worst
* mandātum, mandātī, n. –
      instruction, order
* mandō, mandāre, mandāvī,
      mandātus – order, entrust,
      hand over
* māne – in the morning
* maneō, manēre, mānsī – remain, stay
* manus, manūs, f. – hand; band
      in manum convenīre – pass into
      the hands of
* mare, maris, n. – sea
* marītus, marītī, m. – husband
  marmor, marmoris, n. – marble
  Mārtiālis, Mārtiāle – of Martial
  massa, massae, f. – block
* māter, mātris, f. – mother
  mātrimōnium, mātrimōniī, n. –
      marriage
  maximē see magnopere
  maximus see magnus
  mē see ego
  medicīna, medicīnae, f. – medicine
* medicus, medicī, m. – doctor
* meditor, meditārī, meditātus sum –
      consider
* medius, media, medium – middle
  melior see bonus
  meminī, meminisse – remember
  memor, gen. memoris – remembering,
      mindful of
* mendāx, mendācis, m. – liar
  mendāx, gen. mendācis – lying,
      deceitful
* mēns, mentis, f. – mind
* mēnsa, mēnsae, f. – table
* mēnsis, mēnsis, m. – month
* mentior, mentīrī, mentītus sum – lie,
      tell a lie
* mercātor, mercātōris, m. – merchant
  mereō, merēre, meruī – deserve
*   meritus, merita, meritum –
      deserved, well-deserved

  mergō, mergere, mersī, mersus –
      submerge
  meritō – deservedly, rightly
  metallum, metallī, n. – a mine
* metus, metūs, m. – fear
* meus, mea, meum – my, mine
      mī Lupe – my dear Lupus
  mihi see ego
* mīles, mīlitis, m. – soldier
  mīlitō, mīlitāre, mīlitāvī – be a soldier
* mīlle – a thousand
*   mīlia – thousands
  minae, minārum, f.pl. – threats
* minimē – no, least, very little
  minimus see parvus
  minister, ministrī, m. – servant, agent
  minor see parvus
* minor, minārī, minātus sum + dat. –
      threaten
* mīrābilis, mīrābile – marvelous,
      wonderful
* mīror, mīrārī, mīrātus sum – admire,
      wonder at
  mīrus, mīra, mīrum – extraordinary
* miser, misera, miserum – miserable,
      wretched, sad
* mittō, mittere, mīsī, missus – send
  moderātiō, moderātiōnis, f. –
      moderation, caution
* modo – just, now, only, just now
      nōn modo . . . sed etiam – not only
      . . . but also
* modus, modī, m. – manner, way, kind
*   quō modō? – how? in what way?
  moenia, moeniōrum, n.pl. – city walls
* molestus, molesta, molestum –
      troublesome
  molliō, mollīre, mollīvī, mollītus –
      soothe
  molliter – gently, leniently
* moneō, monēre, monuī, monitus –
      warn, advise
* mōns, montis, m. – mountain
      mōns Palātīnus – the Palatine hill
      summus mōns – the top of the
      mountain

* morbus, morbī, m. – illness
* morior, morī, mortuus sum – die
    morere! – die!
*   mortuus, mortua, mortuum – dead
* moror, morārī, morātus sum – delay
* mors, mortis, f. – death
    mortem sibi cōnscīscere – commit
        suicide
    mortālis, mortāle – mortal
        genus mortāle – the human race
    mortuus see morior
* mōs, mōris, m. – custom
    mōtus, mōtūs, m. – movement
* moveō, movēre, mōvī, mōtus – move,
        influence
* mox – soon
* multitūdō, multitūdinis, f. – crowd
* multō – much
* multus, multa, multum – much
*   multī – many
*   plūrimī, plūrimae, plūrima – very
        many
*   plūrimus, plūrima, plūrimum –
        most
*   plūs, gen. plūris – more
        quid multa? – in brief, in short
    mūniō, mūnīre, mūnīvī, mūnītus –
        protect, immunize
* mūrus, mūrī, m. – wall
    musca, muscae, f. – fly
    musicus, musicī, m. – musician
* mūtō, mūtāre, mūtāvī, mūtātus –
        change
        vestem mūtāre – put on mourning
        clothes

n

* nam – for
    nārrātiō, nārrātiōnis, f. – narration
* nārrō, nārrāre, nārrāvī, nārrātus –
        tell, relate
* nāscor, nāscī, nātus sum – be born
    nātū maximus – eldest
    septuāgintā annōs nātus – seventy
        years old

nat see nō
* (diēs) nātālis, (diēī) nātālis, m. –
        birthday
    natō, natāre, natāvī – swim
    nātus see nāscor
* nauta, nautae, m. – sailor
* nāvigō, nāvigāre, nāvigāvī – sail
* nāvis, nāvis, f. – ship
* nē – that . . . not, in order that . . .
        not
*   nē . . . quidem – not even
    nec – and not, nor
        nec . . . nec – neither . . . nor
* necesse – necessary
* necō, necāre, necāvī, necātus – kill
* neglegēns, gen. neglegentis – careless
* neglegō, neglegere, neglēxī,
        neglēctus – neglect
* negōtium, negōtiī, n. – business
*   negōtium agere – do business,
        work
* nēmō – no one, nobody
    Neptūnus, Neptūnī, m. – Neptune
        (god of the sea)
    neque – and not, nor
*   neque . . . neque – neither . . . nor
* nescio, nescīre, nescīvī – not know
* niger, nigra, nigrum – black
* nihil – nothing
    nihil cūrō – I don't care
* nihilōminus – nevertheless
    nimbus, nimbī, m. – rain-cloud
* nimis – too
* nimium – too much
* nisi – except, unless
    niveus, nivea, niveum – snow-white
    nō, nāre, nāvī – swim
* nōbilis, nōbile – noble, of noble birth
    nōbīs see nōs
* noceō, nocēre, nocuī + dat. – hurt
    nocte see nox
* nōlō, nōlle, nōluī – not want
    nōlī, nōlīte – do not, don't
* nōmen, nōminis, n. – name
    nōminō, nōmināre, nōmināvī,
        nōminātus – name, mention by
        name

* nōn – not
* nōnāgintā – ninety
* nōnne? – surely?
* nōnnūllī, nōnnūllae, nōnnūlla –
    some, several
  nōnnumquam – sometimes
* nōnus, nōna, nōnum – ninth
* nōs – we, us
* noster, nostra, nostrum – our
* nōtus, nōta, nōtum – known,
    well-known, famous
  Notus, Notī, m. – South wind
* novem – nine
* nōvī – I know
* novus, nova, novum – new
* nox, noctis, f. – night
* nūbēs, nūbis, f. – cloud
* nūbō, nūbere, nūpsī + dat. – marry
  nūgae, nūgārum, f.pl. – nonsense,
    foolish talk
* nūllus, nūlla, nūllum – not any, no
* num? – (1) surely . . . not?
* num – (2) whether
* numerō, numerāre, numerāvī,
    numerātus – count
* numerus, numerī, m. – number
* numquam – never
* nunc – now
* nūntiō, nūntiāre, nūntiāvī, nūntiātus
    – announce
* nūntius, nūntiī, m. – messenger,
    message, news
* nūper – recently
  nūptiae, nūptiārum, f.pl. – wedding,
    marriage
  nūptiālis, nūptiāle – wedding,
    marriage
    tabulae nūptiālēs – marriage
    contract, marriage tablets
  nūptūrus see nūbō
* nusquam – nowhere

O

  ob + acc. – on account of, because of

* obiciō, obicere, obiēcī, obiectus –
    present, put in the way of,
    expose to
* oblīvīscor, oblīvīscī, oblītus sum –
    forget
  obscēnus, obscēna, obscēnum –
    obscene, disgusting
* obscūrus, obscūra, obscūrum –
    dark, gloomy
* obstō, obstāre, obstitī + dat. –
    obstruct, block the way
* obstupefaciō, obstupefacere,
    obstupefēcī, obstupefactus –
    amaze, stun
  obtineō, obtinēre, obtinuī, obtentus –
    hold
  obtulī see offerō
* obviam eō, obviam īre, obviam iī
    + dat. – meet, go to meet
* occāsiō, occāsiōnis, f. – opportunity
* occīdō, occīdere, occīdī, occīsus –
    kill
  occidō, occidere, occidī – set
* occupātus, occupāta, occupātum –
    busy
* occupō, occupāre, occupāvī,
    occupātus – seize, take over
* occurrō, occurrere, occurrī – meet
* octāvus, octāva, octāvum – eighth
* octō – eight
* octōgintā – eighty
* oculus, oculī, m. – eye
* ōdī – I hate
  odiōsus, odiōsa, odiōsum – hateful
* odium, odiī, n. – hatred
*   odiō esse – be hateful
* offendō, offendere, offendī, offēnsus –
    displease, offend
* offerō, offerre, obtulī, oblātus – offer
* officium, officiī, n. – duty
    officium agere – do one's duty
  oleum, oleī, n. – oil
* ōlim – once, some time ago
* omnīnō – completely
* omnis, omne – all
    omnia – all, everything
* opēs, opum, f.pl. – money, wealth

* oportet, oportēre, oportuit – be right
  nōs oportet – we must
* oppidum, oppidī, n. – town
* opprimō, opprimere, oppressī,
  oppressus – crush
* oppugnō, oppugnāre, oppugnāvī,
  oppugnātus – attack
  optimē *see* bene
  optimus *see* bonus
* opus, operis, n. – work, construction
* ōrātiō, ōrātiōnis, f. – speech
  ōrātiō solūta – prose speech
  orbis, orbis, m. – globe, world
* ōrdō, ōrdinis, m. – row, line
* orior, orīrī, ortus sum – rise, rise up,
  arise
* ōrnō, ōrnāre, ōrnāvī, ōrnātus –
  decorate
  ōrnātus, ōrnāta, ōrnātum –
  decorated, elaborately furnished
* ōrō, ōrāre, ōrāvī – beg
* ōs, ōris, n. – face
* ōsculum, ōsculī, n. – kiss
* ostendō, ostendere, ostendī,
  ostentus – show
* ōtiōsus, ōtiōsa, ōtiōsum – idle, on
  holiday, on vacation
  ōtium, ōtiī, n. – leisure
  Ovidiānus, Ovidiāna, Ovidiānum
  – of Ovid
  ovis, ovis, f. – sheep

p

pācem *see* pāx
* paene – nearly, almost
  Palātīnus, Palātīna, Palātīnum –
  Palatine
  mōns Palātīnus – the Palatine hill
* pallēscō, pallēscere, palluī – grow
  pale
* pallidus, pallida, pallidum – pale
* pār, *gen.* paris – equal
* parātus, parāta, parātum – ready,
  prepared

* parcō, parcere, pepercī + *dat.* –
  spare
* parēns, parentis, m.f. – parent
* pāreō, pārēre, pāruī + *dat.* – obey
* parō, parāre, parāvī, parātus –
  prepare
* pars, partis, f. – part
* parvus, parva, parvum – small
  minor, *gen.* minōris – less, smaller
* minimus, minima, minimum –
  very little, least
  passus *see* patior
* patefaciō, patefacere, patefēcī,
  patefactus – reveal
* pater, patris, m. – father
* patior, patī, passus sum – suffer,
  endure
* patria, patriae, f. – country,
  homeland
* patrōnus, patrōnī, m. – patron
* paucī, paucae, pauca – few, a few
* paulīsper – for a short time
* paulō – a little
* pauper, *gen.* pauperis – poor
* pavor, pavōris, m. – panic
* pāx, pācis, f. – peace
* pecūnia, pecūniae, f. – money
  pedem *see* pēs
* pendeō, pendēre, pependī – hang
  pepercī *see* parcō
* per + *acc.* – through, along
  percutiō, percutere, percussī,
  percussus – strike
* perdō, perdere, perdidī, perditus –
  destroy
* pereō, perīre, periī – die, perish
* perficiō, perficere, perfēcī, perfectus –
  finish
* perfidia, perfidiae, f. – treachery
* perfidus, perfida, perfidum –
  treacherous, untrustworthy
* perīculōsus, perīculōsa, perīculōsum
  – dangerous
* perīculum, perīculī, n. – danger
  periī *see* pereō
* perītus, perīta, perītum – skillful

* permōtus, permōta, permōtum –
    alarmed, disturbed
* persuādeō, persuādēre, persuāsī
    + *dat.* – persuade
* perterritus, perterrita, perterritum –
    terrified
* perturbō, perturbāre, perturbāvī,
    perturbātus – disturb, alarm
* perveniō, pervenīre, pervēnī –
    reach, arrive at
* pēs, pedis, m. – foot, paw
* pestis, pestis, f. – pest, rascal
* petō, petere, petīvī, petītus – head for,
    attack; seek, beg for, ask for
  phōca, phōcae, f. – seal
  pietās, pietātis, f. – duty
  piscis, piscis, m. – fish
* placeō, placēre, placuī + *dat.* –
    please, suit
* plaudō, plaudere, plausī, plausus –
    applaud, clap
* plaustrum, plaustrī, n. – wagon, cart
  plausus, plausūs, m. – applause
* plēnus, plēna, plēnum – full
* plērīque, plēraeque, plēraque – most,
    the majority
  plūrimī *see* multus
* pōculum, pōculī, n. – cup (often for
    wine)
* poena, poenae, f. – punishment
* poenās dare – pay the penalty, be
    punished
* poēta, poētae, m. – poet
* polliceor, pollicērī, pollicitus sum –
    promise
* pompa, pompae, f. – procession
* pōnō, pōnere, posuī, positus – put,
    place, put up
* pōns, pontis, m. – bridge
* pontifex, pontificis, m. – priest
    Pontifex Maximus – Chief Priest
  pontus, pontī, m. – sea
  poposcī *see* poscō
* populus, populī, m. – people
* porta, portae, f. – gate
* portō, portāre, portāvī, portātus –
    carry

* portus, portūs, m. – harbor
* poscō, poscere, poposcī – demand,
    ask for
  possideō, possidēre, possēdī,
    possessus – possess
* possum, posse, potuī – can, be able
* post + *acc.* – after, behind
* posteā – afterwards
  postis, postis, m. – door, door-post
* postquam – after, when
* postrēmō – finally, lastly
* postrīdiē – on the next day
* postulō, postulāre, postulāvī,
    postulātus – demand
  posuī *see* pōnō
* potēns, *gen.* potentis – powerful
  potes *see* possum
* potestās, potestātis, f. – power
    in potestātem redigere – bring
    under the control
* praebeō, praebēre, praebuī,
    praebitus – provide
* praeceps, *gen.* praecipitis – headlong
  praecipitō, praecipitāre, praecipitāvī
    – hurl
* praecō, praecōnis, m. – herald,
    announcer
* praefectus, praefectī, m. –
    commander
    praefectus praetōriō – commander
    of the praetorian guard
* praeficiō, praeficere, praefēcī,
    praefectus – put in charge
* praemium, praemiī, n. – prize,
    reward, profit
* praesēns, *gen.* praesentis – present,
    ready
* praesertim – especially
* praesidium, praesidiī, n. – protection
* praestō, praestāre, praestitī – show,
    display
* praesum, praeesse, praefuī + *dat.* – be
    in charge of
* praeter + *acc.* – except
* praytereā – besides
* praetereō, praeterīre, praeteriī –
    pass by, go past

175

praetōriānus, praetōriāna,
praetōriānum – praetorian
(belonging to emperor's
bodyguard)
praetōrium, praetōriī, n. – the
praetorian guard
praefectus praetōriō – commander
of the praetorian guard
* prāvus, prāva, prāvum – evil
* precēs, precum, f.pl. – prayers
* precor, precārī, precātus sum – pray
(to)
prēnsō, prēnsāre, prēnsāvī,
prēnsātus – take hold of, clutch
* pretiōsus, pretiōsa, pretiōsum –
expensive, precious
* pretium, pretiī, n. – price
prīdiē – the day before
prīmō – at first
prīmum – first
cum prīmum – as soon as
* prīmus, prīma, prīmum – first
* prīnceps, prīncipis, m. – chief,
chieftain, emperor
prīncipātus, prīncipātūs, m. –
principate, reign
* prīncipia, prīncipiōrum, n.pl. –
headquarters
* prior, prius – in front, earlier
* priusquam – before, until
prīvātus, prīvāta, prīvātum – private
* prō + abl. – in front of, for, in return
for
* prō certō habēre – know for certain
* probō, probāre, probāvī – prove
* prōcēdō, prōcēdere, prōcessī –
advance, proceed
* procul – far off
* prōcumbō, prōcumbere, prōcubuī –
fall down
* prōdō, prōdere, prōdidī, prōditus –
betray
* proelium, proeliī, n. – battle
* proficīscor, proficīscī, profectus sum
– set out
* prōgredior, prōgredī, prōgressus sum
– advance

* prohibeō, prohibēre, prohibuī,
prohibitus – prevent
* prōmittō, prōmittere, prōmīsī,
prōmissus – promise
prōnūntiō, prōnūntiāre, prōnūntiāvī,
prōnūntiātus – proclaim,
preach, announce
* prope – near
properō, properāre, properāvī –
hurry
prōpōnō, prōpōnere, prōposuī,
prōpositus – propose, put
forward
propter + acc. – because of
prōtinus – immediately
* prōvincia, prōvinciae, f. – province
* proximus, proxima, proximum –
nearest, next to, last
prūdēns, gen. prūdentis – shrewd,
intelligent, sensible
prūdenter – prudently, sensibly
* prūdentia, prūdentiae, f. – prudence,
good sense, shrewdness
pūblicō, pūblicāre, pūblicāvī,
pūblicātus – confiscate
* pūblicus, pūblica, pūblicum – public
* puella, puellae, f. – girl
* puer, puerī, m. – boy
pugiō, pugiōnis, m. – dagger
* pugna, pugnae, f. – fight
* pugnō, pugnāre, pugnāvī – fight
* pulcher, pulchra, pulchrum –
beautiful
* pulsō, pulsāre, pulsāvī, pulsātus – hit,
knock at, thump, punch
pūmiliō, pūmiliōnis, m. – dwarf
* pūniō, pūnīre, pūnīvī, pūnītus –
punish
* puto, putāre, putāvī – think

q

Q. = Quīntus
quā – where
* quadrāgintā – forty
quadrīga, quadrīgae, f. – chariot

quaedam *see* quīdam

* quaerō, quaerere, quaesīvī, quaesītus
    – search for, look for

quaesō – I beg, i.e. please

* quālis, quāle – what sort of
* quam – (1) how
* quam – (2) than
    quam celerrimē – as quickly as
        possible
* quamquam – although
* quandō? – when?
* quantus, quanta, quantum – how big
* quārē? – why?
* quartus, quārta, quārtum   fourth
* quasi – as if
* quattuor – four
* quattuordecim – fourteen
* -que – and
quendam *see* quīdam
querēla, querēlae, f. – complaint
* queror, querī, questus sum – lament,
    complain about
* quī, quae, quod – who, which
    id quod – what
    quod sī – but if
quī? quae? quod? – which? what?
* quia – because
* quicquam (*also spelt* quidquam) –
    anything
quicquid – whatever
quīcumque, quaecumque,
    quodcumque – whoever,
    whatever, any whatever
quid? *see* quis?
* quīdam, quaedam, quoddam – one, a
    certain
* quidem – indeed
*   ne . . . quidem – not even
* quiēs, quiētis, f. – rest
* quīndecim – fifteen
* quīnquāgintā – fifty
* quīnque – five
* quīntus, quīnta, quīntum – fifth
* quis? quid? – who? what?
    quid agis? – how are you? how are
        you doing?
    quid faciam? – what am I to do?

quid multa? – in brief, in short
* quō? – where? where to?
* quō modō? – how? in what way?
* quod – because
    ideō quod – for the reason that,
        because
quōdam *see* quīdam
* quondam – one day, once
* quoque – also, too
quōsdam *see* quīdam
* quot? – how many?
* quotiēns – whenever

r

* rapiō, rapere, rapuī, raptus – seize,
    grab
rārō – rarely
ratiō, ratiōnis, f. – reason
* ratiōnēs, ratiōnum, f.pl. – accounts
rē *see* rēs
rebellō, rebellāre, rebellāvī – rebel,
    revolt
rēbus *see* rēs
* recipiō, recipere, recēpī, receptus –
    recover, take back
recitātiō, recitātiōnis, f. – recital,
    public reading
* recitō, recitāre, recitāvī, recitātus –
    recite, read out
* rēctē – rightly, properly
* recumbō, recumbere, recubuī – lie
    down, recline
* recūsō, recūsāre, recūsāvī, recūsātus
    – refuse
* reddō, reddere, reddidī, redditus –
    give back, make
* redeō, redīre, rediī – return, go back,
    come back
redigō, redigere, redēgī, redāctus
    – bring
    in potestātem redigere – bring
        under the control
* redūcō, redūcere, redūxī, reductus –
    lead back

* referō, referre, rettulī, relātus –
    bring back, carry, deliver, tell,
    report
    victōriam referre – win a victory
* reficiō, reficere, refēcī, refectus –
    repair
* rēgīna, rēgīnae, f. – queen
* regiō, regiōnis, f. – region
    rēgis see rēx
* rēgnum, rēgnī, n. – kingdom
* regō, regere, rēxī, rēctus – rule
* regredior, regredī, regressus sum –
    go back, return
    reiciō, reicere, reiēcī, reiectus – reject
* relēgō, relēgāre, relēgāvī, relēgātus –
    exile
* relinquō, relinquere, relīquī,
    relictus – leave
    reliquiae, reliquiārum, f.pl. – remains
    rem see rēs
* remedium, remediī, n. – cure
    rēmigō, rēmigāre, rēmigāvī – row
    rēmus, rēmī, m. – oar
    renovō, renovāre, renovāvī,
        renovātus – renew, repeat,
        resume
    repente – suddenly
    reperiō, reperīre, repperī, repertus –
        find
    reprehendō, reprehendere,
        reprehendī, reprehēnsus –
        blame, criticize
    repudiō, repudiāre, repudiāvī,
        repudiātus – divorce
* rēs, reī, f. – thing, business
*   rē vērā – in fact, truly, really
    rem cōgitāre – consider the
        problem
    rem nārrāre – tell the story
*   rēs adversae – misfortune
* resistō, resistere, restitī + dat. – resist
* respiciō, respicere, respexī – look at,
    look back, look up
* respondeō, respondēre, respondī –
    reply
    respōnsum, respōnsī, n. – answer

    restituō, restituere, restituī,
        restitūtus – restore
    resūmō, resūmere, resūmpsī,
        resūmptus – pick up again
* retineō, retinēre, retinuī,
    retentus – keep, hold back
    rettulī see referō
* reveniō, revenīre, revēnī – come back,
    return
* revertor, revertī, reversus sum – turn
    back, return
* revocō, revocāre, revocāvī, revocātus
    – recall, call back
* rēx, rēgis, m. – king
    rēxī see regō
    rhētor, rhētoris, m. – teacher
* rīdeō, rīdēre, rīsī – laugh, smile
    rīdiculus, rīdicula, rīdiculum –
        ridiculous, silly
* rīpa, rīpae, f. – river bank
    rīsus, rīsūs, m. – smile
* rogō, rogāre, rogāvī, rogātus – ask
    Rōma, Rōmae, f. – Rome
        Rōmae – at Rome
    Rōmānī, Rōmānōrum, m.pl. –
        Romans
    Rōmānus, Rōmāna, Rōmānum –
        Roman
    ruīna, ruīnae, f. – ruin, wreckage
* ruō, ruere, ruī – rush
* rūrsus – again
* rūs, rūris, n. – country, countryside
    rūsticus, rūstica, rūsticum –
        country, in the country
    vīlla rūstica – house in the country

S

* sacer, sacra, sacrum – sacred
* sacerdōs, sacerdōtis, m. – priest
    sacerdōtium, sacerdōtiī, n. –
        priesthood
    sacrificium, sacrificiī, n. – offering,
        sacrifice

sacrificō, sacrificāre, sacrificāvī,
    sacrificātus – sacrifice
* saepe – often
* saeviō, saevīre, saeviī – be in a rage
* saevus, saeva, saevum – savage, cruel
* saltō, saltāre, saltāvī – dance
* salūs, salūtis, f. – safety, health
    salūtem dīcere – sends good wishes
* salūtō, salūtāre, salūtāvī, salūtātus –
    greet
* salvē! salvēte! – hello!
* sānē – obviously
* sanguis, sanguinis, m. – blood
  sānō, sānāre, sānāvī, sānātus – heal,
    cure, treat
* sapiēns, *gen.* sapientis – wise
  sapienter – wisely
* satis – enough
*   satis cōnstat – it is generally agreed
* saxum, saxī, n. – rock
  scaena, scaenae, f. – stage, scene
    extrēma scaena – the edge of the
    stage
* scelestus, scelesta, scelestum –
    wicked
* scelus, sceleris, n. – crime
  scīlicet – obviously
* scindō, scindere, scidī, scissus – tear,
    tear up, cut up
* scio, scīre, scīvī – know
* scrībō, scrībere, scrīpsī, scrīptus –
    write
  sculptor, sculptōris, m. – sculptor
  scurrīlis, scurrīle – gross, obscene
* sē – himself, herself, themselves
    inter sē – among themselves, with
    each other
* secō, secāre, secuī, sectus – cut
  sēcrētus, sēcrēta, sēcrētum – secret
* secundus, secunda, secundum –
    second
  secūris, secūris, f. – axe
* sēcūrus, sēcūra, sēcūrum – without a
    care
  secūtus *see* sequor
* sed – but

* sēdecim – sixteen
* sedeō, sedēre, sēdī – sit
* sēdēs, sēdis, f. – seat
  sēdō, sēdāre, sēdāvī, sēdātus – quell,
    calm down
  seges, segetis, f. – crop, harvest
  sēiūnctus, sēiūncta, sēiūnctum –
    separate
* sella, sellae, f. – chair
* semper – always
* senātor, senātōris, m. – senator
  senātus, senātūs, m. – senate
    cognitiō senātūs – trial by the
    senate
* senex, senis, m. – old man
  sēnsus, sēnsūs, m. – feeling
* sententia, sententiae, f. – opinion,
    sentence
* sentiō, sentīre, sēnsī, sēnsus – feel,
    notice
* septem – seven
* septendecim – seventeen
* septimus, septima, septimum –
    seventh
* septuāgintā – seventy
* sepulcrum, sepulcrī, n. – tomb
* sequor, sequī, secūtus sum – follow
* serēnus, serēna, serēnum – calm,
    clear
* sermō, sermōnis, m. – conversation
* serviō, servīre, servīvī + *dat.* – serve
    (as a slave)
* servō, servāre, servāvī, servātus –
    save, look after
* servus, servī, m. – slave
  sevērē – severely
* sevērus, sevēra, sevērum – severe,
    strict
* sex – six
* sexāgintā – sixty
* sextus, sexta, sextum – sixth
* sī – if
    quod sī – but if
  sibi *see* sē
  sibilō, sibilāre, sibilāvī – hiss
* sīc – thus, in this way

* sīcut – like
  sīcut . . . ita – just as . . . so
sīdus, sīderis, n. – star
significō, significāre, significāvī,
    significātus – mean, indicate
signō, signāre, signāvī, signātus –
    sign, seal
* signum, signī, n. – sign, seal, signal
* silentium, silentiī, n. – silence
* silva, silvae, f. – wood, forest
  sim see sum
* similis, simile – similar
* simul – at the same time
* simulac, simulatque – as soon as
* simulō, simulāre, simulāvī,
    simulātus – pretend
* sine + abl. – without
  sistō, sistere, stitī – stop, halt
  socia, sociae, f. – companion, partner
* socius, sociī, m. – companion, partner
* sōl, sōlis, m. – sun
* soleō, solēre – be accustomed
  sollemnis, sollemne – solemn,
    traditional
  sollemniter – solemnly
  sollicitō, sollicitāre, sollicitāvī,
    sollicitātus – worry
  sollicitūdō, sollicitūdinis, f. – anxiety
* sollicitus, sollicita, sollicitum –
    worried, anxious
* sōlus, sōla, sōlum – alone, lonely,
    only, on one's own
* solvō, solvere, solvī, solūtus – loosen,
    untie, cast off
  ōrātiō solūta – prose speech
* sonitus, sonitūs, m. – sound
* sordidus, sordida, sordidum – dirty
* soror, sorōris, f. – sister
* sors, sortis, f. – lot
* spargō, spargere, sparsī, sparsus –
    scatter
  spē see spēs
  speciēs, speciēī, f. – appearance
  speciōsus, speciōsa, speciōsum –
    impressive
* spectāculum, spectāculī, n. – show,
    spectacle

spectātor, spectātōris, m. – spectator
* spectō, spectāre, spectāvī, spectātus –
    look at, watch
* spernō, spernere, sprēvī, sprētus –
    despise, reject, ignore
* spērō, spērāre, spērāvī – hope, expect
* spēs, speī, f. – hope
  splendidus, splendida, splendidum –
    splendid, impressive
  sportula, sportulae, f. – handout (gift
    of food or money)
  st! – hush!
  stābam see stō
* statim – at once
* statiō, statiōnis, f. – post
  statua, statuae, f. – statue
* stilus, stilī, m. – pen (pointed stick for
    writing on wax tablet)
* stō, stāre, stetī – stand, lie at anchor
* stola, stolae, f. – (long) dress
* strēnuē – hard, energetically
* strepitus, strepitūs, m. – noise, din
* studium, studiī, n. – enthusiasm;
    study
* stultus, stulta, stultum – stupid, foolish
* suādeō, suādēre, suāsī + dat. –
    advise, suggest
* suāvis, suāve – sweet
* suāviter – sweetly
* sub + abl. – under, beneath
* subitō – suddenly
* subveniō, subvenīre, subvēnī + dat. –
    help, come to help
* sum, esse, fuī – be
    estō! – be!
* summus, summa, summum –
    highest, greatest, top
  summus mōns – the top of the
    mountain
  sūmō, sūmere, sūmpsī, sūmptus –
    take
* sūmptuōsus, sūmptuōsa,
    sūmptuōsum – expensive,
    lavish, costly
  superbē – arrogantly
* superbus, superba, superbum –
    arrogant, proud

supercilia, superciliōrum, n.pl. –
    eyebrows
  supercilia contrahere – draw
    eyebrows together, frown
* superō, superāre, superāvī, superātus
    – overcome, overpower
  superpōnō, superpōnere, superposuī,
    superpositus – place on
  superstes, superstitis, m. – survivor
* supersum, superesse, superfuī –
    survive
  suppliciter – like a suppliant, humbly
* supplicium, suppliciī, n. –
    punishment, penalty
  supplicium ultimum – death
    penalty
  supprimō, supprimere, suppressī,
    suppressus – staunch, stop flow
* suprā + acc. – over, on top of
* surgō, surgere, surrēxī – get up, rise
* suscipiō, suscipere, suscēpī,
    susceptus – undertake, take on
  suspīciō, suspīciōnis, f. – suspicion
* suspicor, suspicārī, suspicātus sum –
    suspect
  sustulī *see* tollere
  susurrō, susurrāre, susurrāvī –
    whisper, mumble
* suus, sua, suum – his, her, their, his
    own

t

T. = Titus
* taberna, tabernae, f. – store, inn
  tablīnum, tablīnī, n. – study
  tabula, tabulae, f. – tablet,
    writing-tablet
  tabulae nūptiālēs – marriage
    contract, marriage tablets
* taceō, tacēre, tacuī – be silent, be
    quiet
  tacē! – shut up! be quiet!
* tacitē – quietly, silently
* tacitus, tacita, tacitum – quiet, silent,
    in silence

* taedet, taedēre – be tiring
* tālis, tāle – such
* tam – so
* tamen – however
* tamquam – as, like
* tandem – at last
* tangō, tangere, tetigī, tāctus – touch
* tantum – only
* tantus, tanta, tantum – so great, such
    a great
  tantī esse – be worth
* tardus, tarda, tardum – late
  tē *see* tū
* tēctum, tēctī, n. – ceiling, roof
  tellūs, tellūris, f. – land, earth
* tempestās, tempestātis, f. – storm
* templum, templī, n. – temple
* temptō, temptāre, temptāvī,
    temptātus – try, put to the test
* tempus, temporis, n. – time
* tenebrae, tenebrārum, f.pl. –
    darkness
* teneō, tenēre, tenuī, tentus – hold
* tergum, tergī, n. – back
* terra, terrae, f. – ground, land
* terreō, terrēre, terruī, territus –
    frighten
* tertius, tertia, tertium – third
* testāmentum, testāmentī, n. – will
  testimōnium, testimōniī, n. –
    evidence
* testis, testis, m.f. – witness
  testor, testārī, testātus sum – call to
    witness
  tetigī *see* tangere
  theātrum, theātrī, n. – theater
  thermae, thermārum, f.pl. – baths
  Tiberis, Tiberis, m. – river Tiber
  tibi *see* tū
  tībia, tībiae, f. – pipe
* timeō, timēre, timuī – be afraid, fear
  timidus, timida, timidum – fearful,
    frightened
* timor, timōris, m. – fear
  toga, togae, f. – toga
* tollō, tollere, sustulī, sublātus – raise,
    lift up, hold up; remove, do
    away with

tormentum, tormentī, n. – torture
torqueō, torquēre, torsī, tortus –
   torture, twist
* tot – so many
* tōtus, tōta, tōtum – whole
* trādō, trādere, trādidī, trāditus –
   hand over
* trahō, trahere, trāxī, tractus – drag
* trāns + *acc.* – across
* trānseō, trānsīre, trānsiī – cross
* trēdecim – thirteen
tremō, tremere, tremuī – tremble,
   shake
* trēs, tria – three
* tribūnus, tribūnī, m. – tribune
    (high-ranking officer)
tribūtum, tribūtī, n. – tribute, tax
triclīnium, triclīniī, n. – dining-room
tridēns, tridentis, m. – trident
* trīgintā – thirty
* trīstis, trīste – sad
triumphus, triumphī, m. – triumph
   triumphum agere – celebrate a
    triumph
* tū, tuī – you (singular)
* tuba, tubae, f. – trumpet
tulī *see* ferō
* tum – then
*   tum dēmum – then at last, only
   then
* tumultus, tumultī, m. – riot
* turba, turbae, f. – crowd
turpis, turpe – shameful
* tūtus, tūta, tūtum – safe
* tuus, tua, tuum – your (singular),
   yours

u

* ubi – where, when
* ubīque – everywhere
* ūllus, ūlla, ūllum – any
ulmus, ulmī, f. – elm-tree
* ultimus, ultima, ultimum – furthest,
   last

supplicium ultimum – death
   penalty
* ultiō, ultiōnis, f. – revenge
* umbra, umbrae, f. – shadow, ghost
* umerus, umerī, m. – shoulder
* umquam – ever
* unda, undae, f. – wave
* unde – from where
* ūndecim – eleven
* ūndēvīgintī – nineteen
* undique – on all sides
* unguō, unguere, ūnxī, ūnctus –
   anoint, smear
* ūnus, ūna, ūnum – one
* urbs, urbis, f. – city
ūsus, ūsūs, m. – use
   ūsuī esse – be of use
* ut – (1) as
* ut – (2) that, so that, in order that
uterque, utraque, utrumque – each,
   both
* ūtilis, ūtile – useful
* ūtor, ūtī, ūsus sum – use
* utrum – whether
*   utrum . . . an – whether . . . or
* uxor, uxōris, f. – wife
   uxōrem dūcere – take as a wife,
    marry

v

* vacuus, vacua, vacuum – empty
vagor, vagārī, vagātus sum – spread,
   go round
vagus, vaga, vagum – wandering
* valdē – very much, very
* valē – good-by
valedīcō, valedīcere, valedīxī – say
   good-by
* validus, valida, validum – strong
* vehementer – violently, loudly
* vehō, vehere, vexī, vectus – carry
* vel – or
velim *see* volō
vēna, vēnae, f. – vein
* vēnātiō, vēnātiōnis, f. – hunt

* vēndō, vēndere, vēndidī,
    vēnditus – sell
* venēnum, venēnī, n. – poison
* venia, veniae, f. – mercy
* veniō, venīre, vēnī – come
  vēnor, vēnārī, vēnātus sum – hunt
* ventus, ventī, m. – wind
  venustās, venustātis, f. – charm
* verberō, verberāre, verberāvī,
    verberātus – strike, beat
* verbum, verbī, n. – word
* vereor, verērī, veritus sum – be afraid,
    fear
* vērō – indeed
  versus, versūs, m. – verse, line of
    poetry
  vertex, verticis, m. – top, peak
* vertō, vertere, vertī, versus – turn
    sē vertere – turn round
* vērum, vērī, n. – truth
* vērus, vēra, vērum – true, real
*   rē vērā – in fact, truly, really
  vespillō, vespillōnis, m. – undertaker
* vester, vestra, vestrum – your
    (plural)
* vestīmenta, vestīmentōrum, n.pl. –
    clothes
* vestis, vestis, f. – clothing
    vestem mūtāre – put on mourning
    clothes
* vetus, *gen.* veteris – old
* vexō, vexāre, vexāvī, vexātus – annoy
* via, viae, f. – street, way
* vīcīnus, vīcīnī, m. – neighbor
  victima, victimae, f. – victim
* victor, victōris, m. – victor, winner
  victōria, victōriae, f. – victory
    victōriam referre – win a victory
  victus *see* vincere
* videō, vidēre, vīdī, vīsus – see
* videor, vidērī, vīsus sum – seem
* vīgintī – twenty
  vīlis, vīle – cheap
* vīlla, vīllae, f. – villa, (large) house
* vinciō, vincīre, vīnxī, vīnctus – bind,
    tie up

* vincō, vincere, vīcī, victus – conquer,
    win, be victorious
  vindicō, vindicāre, vindicāvī,
    vindicātus – avenge
* vīnum, vīnī, n. – wine
* vir, virī, m. – man
* virgō, virginis, f. – virgin
* virtūs, virtūtis, f. – courage, virtue
  vīs *see* volō
  vīsitō, vīsitāre, vīsitāvī, vīsitātus –
    visit
  vīsus *see* videō
* vīta, vītae, f. – life
  vītam agere – lead a life
* vītō, vītāre, vītāvī, vītātus – avoid
* vituperō, vituperāre, vituperāvī,
    vituperātus – find fault with,
    curse
* vīvō, vīvere, vīxī – live, be alive
* vīvus, vīva, vīvum – alive, living
* vix – hardly, scarcely, with difficulty
  vōbīs *see* vōs
  vōcem *see* vōx
* vocō, vocāre, vocāvī, vocātus – call
* volō, velle, voluī – want
  velim – I should like
  volucris, volucris, f. – bird
* volvō, volvere, volvī, volūtus – turn
*   in animō volvere – wonder, turn
    over in the mind
* vōs – you (plural)
  vōbīscum – with you (plural)
* vōx, vōcis, f. – voice
* vulnerō, vulnerāre, vulnerāvī,
    vulnerātus – wound, injure
* vulnus, vulneris, n. – wound
  vult *see* volō
* vultus, vultūs, m. – expression, face

Guide to characters and places in Unit IVA

(The numeral in brackets identifies the Stage in which the person(s) or place is/
are first featured.)

Gnaeus Iūlius AGRICOLA (35): Roman governor of Britain in A.D. 78–84 (see
  Unit IIIA); victorious over Caledonians in A.D. 84; recalled by Emperor
  Domitian.
Gāius Valerius CATULLUS (36): Roman lyric poet (84–54 B.C.).
Titus Flāvius CLĒMĒNS (38): senator; father of Polla, Publius and Titus;
  executed, with Glabrio, for atheism (or Christianity) in A.D. 95.
Tiberius Claudius COGIDUBNUS (40): client-king of Regnenses (see Units IIA
  and IIIA); Salvius was accused of having poisoned him and forged his will.
Quīntus Vibius CRISPUS (37): senator and ex-consul; oldest of Domitian's
  private counselors.
DOMITIA Augusta (40): wife of Domitian (see Unit IIIB); recalled from exile.
Titus Flāvius DOMITIĀNUS (35): Domitian, Emperor of Rome in A.D. 81–96
  (see Unit IIIB), also called by title 'Augustus'; celebrated triumph over
  Germanic Chatti (in modern Hesse); punished Vestal Virgins; as Pontifex
  Maximus, celebrated Polla's marriage to Sparsus; adopted Publius and Titus;
  recalled exiled wife Domitia.
Claudius EPAPHRODĪTUS (37): freedman; secretary to Domitian (see Unit
  IIIB); his power was feared by senators.
FLĀVIA Domitilla (38): granddaughter of Vespasian and related to Domitian;
  mother of Polla, Publius and Titus.
Pūblius Cornēlius FUSCUS (37): commander of praetorian guard; opposed
  Agricola at emperor's council.
Servius Sulpicius GALBA (37): like Agricola, was governor of a province
  (Hispania Tarraconensis) for seven years; revolted against the Roman state,
  and was declared emperor (A.D. 68–9).
Mānius Acīlius GLABRIŌ (35): wrote critically about the emperor to Lupus;
  walked out of recitatio when poet Martial praised Domitian; supported
  Agricola at emperor's council; accused Salvius of forgery; rewarded with
  priesthood by Domitian.
Quīntus HATERIUS Latrōniānus (40): client and brother-in-law of Salvius (see
  Unit IIIB); voluntarily went into exile with Salvius.
Helvidius (35): fifteen-year-old son of C. Helvidius Lupus; liked girls and
  chariots; loved Polla; tried to kill Sparsus but was overpowered and taken away
  to be punished by Domitian.
Iūnō (38): Juno, wife of Jupiter; patron-goddess of marriage.
Iuppiter (39): Jupiter, also called Jove; high god of the Romans; once caused a
  great flood to punish mortals.
Gāius Helvidius LUPUS (35): friend of Glabrio; spent leisure in the country;
  father of young Helvidius.
Marcus Valerius MĀRTIĀLIS (36): Martial, a Roman satirical poet (c. A.D.
  40–104); read his epigrams aloud at a recitatio.

Lūcius Marcius MEMOR (40): haruspex and client of Salvius (see Unit IIIA); betrayed Salvius.

Lūcius Catullus MESSĀLĪNUS (37): one of Domitian's private counselors.

Myropnoüs (40): dwarf; pipe-player friend of Paris (see Unit IIIB); informed on Salvius; refused offer of freedom from Domitian.

Pūblius OVIDIUS Nāsō (39): Ovid, a Roman poet (43 B.C. – A.D. 14); author of mythological epic, *Metamorphoses*, studied by Publius and Titus.

Mōns PALĀTĪNUS (36): the Palatine hill, where Domitian's great palace was built.

Pōlla (38): fourteen-year-old daughter of Clemens and Flavia; loved Helvidius but was married, at emperor's will, to Sparsus.

Publius (38): younger son of Clemens and Flavia, and brother of Polla and Titus; adopted and made heir by Domitian; taught by Quintilian.

Marcus Fabius QUĪNTILIĀNUS (38): Roman rhetor (c. A.D. 35–100); tutor to Publius and Titus; disliked Epaphroditus.

QUĪNTUS Caccilius Iūcundus (40): (see also Units I, IIA, IIB and IIIA); made serious charges against Salvius; rewarded with emperor's favor in seeking public office.

Rūfilla (40): noble-born wife of Salvius (see Unit IIA); promised to stay with him, but later went back to her father's house.

Titus Flāvius SABĪNUS (38): consul in A.D. 82 (see Unit IIIB); brother of Clemens; husband of the Emperor Titus' daughter Julia; executed by order of Domitian.

Gāius SALVIUS Līberālis (40): senator, lawyer and later consul (see Units IIA and IIIA); accused by Glabrio; instigated Paris' death and Domitia's exile; attempted suicide, but was rescued by order of Domitian and then exiled.

Lūcius Ursus SERVIĀNUS (40): senator; presided over Salvius' trial; pronounced him guilty.

Sparsus (38): fifty-five-year-old senator; twice divorced; married young Polla.

Titus (38): older son of Clemens and Flavia, and brother of Polla and Publius; adopted and made heir by Domitian; taught by Quintilian; stuttered.

Aulus Fabricius VĒIENTŌ (37): boldest of Domitian's private counselors.

Titus Flāvius Sabīnus VESPASIĀNUS (35): Vespasian, Emperor of Rome in A.D. 69–79; father of the Emperors Titus and Domitian; grandfather of Flavia; exiled, then executed the father of Lupus.

Virginēs Vestālēs (35): the Vestal Virgins, priestesses of Vesta, goddess of hearth and home; three were condemned to burial alive by Domitian in A.D. 83.

Vitelliānus (40): son of Salvius and Rufilla; advised father to renew his defense; was spared at Salvius' request; received part of his exiled father's property.